PowerPoint 2003

VISUAL™

Quick Tips

Visual

by Nancy Buchanan

WILEY

Wiley Publishing, Inc.

PowerPoint® 2003 Visual Quick Tips

Published by
Wiley Publishing, Inc.
111 River Street
Hoboken, NJ 07030-5774

Copyright © 2006 by Wiley Publishing, Inc.,
Indianapolis, Indiana

Library of Congress Control Number: 2005937797

ISBN: 0-470-00927-6

ISBN13: 978-0-470-00927-7

Manufactured in the United States of America

10 9 8 7 6 5 4 3 2 1

1K/SQ/RS/QV/IN

Trademark Acknowledgments

Contact Us

For general information on our other products and services contact our Customer Care Department within the U.S. at 800-762-2974, outside the U.S. at 317-572-3993 or fax 317-572-4002.

For technical support please visit www.wiley.com/techsupport.

WILEY

Wiley Publishing, Inc.

Sales

Contact Wiley
at (800) 762-2974 or
fax (317) 572-4002.

Praise for Visual Books

"I have to praise you and your company on the fine products you turn out. I have twelve Visual books in my house. They were instrumental in helping me pass a difficult computer course. Thank you for creating books that are easy to follow. Keep turning out those quality books."

Gordon Justin (Brielle, NJ)

"What fantastic teaching books you have produced! Congratulations to you and your staff. You deserve the Nobel prize in Education. Thanks for helping me understand computers."

Bruno Tonon (Melbourne, Australia)

"A Picture Is Worth A Thousand Words! If your learning method is by observing or hands-on training, this is the book for you!"

Lorri Pegan-Durastante (Wickliffe, OH)

"Over time, I have bought a number of your 'Read Less - Learn More' books. For me, they are THE way to learn anything easily. I learn easiest using your method of teaching."

José A. Mazón (Cuba, NY)

"You've got a fan for life!! Thanks so much!!"

Kevin P. Quinn (Oakland, CA)

"I have several books from the Visual series and have always found them to be valuable resources."

Stephen P. Miller (Ballston Spa, NY)

"I have several of your Visual books and they are the best I have ever used."

Stanley Clark (Crawfordville, FL)

"Like a lot of other people, I understand things best when I see them visually. Your books really make learning easy and life more fun."

John T. Frey (Cadillac, MI)

"I have quite a few of your Visual books and have been very pleased with all of them. I love the way the lessons are presented!"

Mary Jane Newman (Yorba Linda, CA)

"Thank you, thank you, thank you...for making it so easy for me to break into this high-tech world."

Gay O'Donnell (Calgary, Alberta, Canada)

"I write to extend my thanks and appreciation for your books. They are clear, easy to follow, and straight to the point. Keep up the good work! I bought several of your books and they are just right! No regrets! I will always buy your books because they are the best."

Seward Kollie (Dakar, Senegal)

"I would like to take this time to thank you and your company for producing great and easy-to-learn products. I bought two of your books from a local bookstore, and it was the best investment I've ever made! Thank you for thinking of us ordinary people."

Jeff Eastman (West Des Moines, IA)

"Compliments to the chef!! Your books are extraordinary! Or, simply put, extra-ordinary, meaning way above the rest! THANKYOU THANKYOU THANKYOU! I buy them for friends, family, and colleagues."

Christine J. Manfrin (Castle Rock, CO)

Credits

Project Editor
Courtney Allen

Acquisitions Editor
Jody Lefevere

Product Development Supervisor
Courtney Allen

Copy Editor
Dana Lesh
Jill Mazurczyk

Technical Editor
Allen Wyatt

Editorial Manager
Robyn Siesky

Editorial Assistant
Adrienne D. Porter

Manufacturing
Allan Conley
Linda Cook
Paul Gilchrist
Jennifer Guynn

Book Design
Kathie S. Rickard

Production Coordinator
Kristie Rees

Layout
Jennifer Heleine

Screen Artist
Elizabeth Cardenas-Nelson
Jill Proll

Illustrators
Ronda David-Burroughs

Cover Design
Anthony Bunyan

Proofreaders
Laura Albert
Robert Springer
Brian Walls

Indexer
Joan Griffiths

Vice President and Executive Group Publisher
Richard Swadley

Vice President Publisher
Barry Pruett

Composition Director
Debbie Stailey

About the Author

Nancy Buchanan is a freelance high-tech marketing consultant and writer who has been in technical marketing and sales for more than 20 years. She was in product marketing for almost eight years at Microsoft Corporation, where she was a product manager for Microsoft Office, for Microsoft FrontPage, and for Windows-based streaming media. She was also responsible for marketing Microsoft products sold to attorneys. Prior to joining Microsoft, Nancy was in sales and marketing for over six years at Novell, Inc. Nancy holds a Bachelor of Arts degree in business administration from University of Washington in Seattle and lives in Washington State with her husband, Doug, and her four children.

How To Use This Book

PowerPoint 2003 Visual Quick Tips includes tasks that reveal cool secrets, teach timesaving tricks, and explain great tips guaranteed to make you more productive with PowerPoint 2003. The easy-to-use layout lets you work through all the tasks from beginning to end or jump in at random.

Who Is This Book For?

You already know PowerPoint 2003 basics. Now you'd like to go beyond, with shortcuts, tricks and tips that let you work smarter and faster. And because you learn more easily when someone *shows* you how, this is the book for you.

Conventions Used In This Book

❶ Steps

This book uses step-by-step instructions to guide you easily through each task. Numbered callouts on every screen shot show you exactly how to perform each task, step by step.

❷ Tips

Practical tips provide insights to save you time and trouble, caution you about hazards to avoid, and reveal how to do things in PowerPoint 2003 that you never thought possible!

Table of Contents

chapter 1
Customize PowerPoint Options to Suit Your Needs

chapter 2
Give Your Presentation the Look You Want

chapter 5   Add Sizzle to Your Presentation with Effects

chapter 6   Communicate with Audio and Video

chapter 7 Enhance Your Presentations with Custom Content

chapter 8 Expand Your Audience by Publishing to the Web

chapter 9 **Collaborate with Others**

chapter 10 **Deliver and Distribute Your Presentation Effectively**

Customize PowerPoint Options to Suit Your Needs

You can get more done faster with PowerPoint 2003 when you customize its options to suit your needs. The tasks in this chapter are geared toward making the PowerPoint user interface work for you by helping you to place the tools you need where you need them.

If you have ever wondered how to open presentations with the Outline tab showing or with the Notes Page hidden, find out how here. It only takes a few minutes to configure PowerPoint to open presentations in the view in which you are most comfortable.

If you are tired of browsing to file folders many levels deep to find or save files, you can save time by adding a shortcut to the My Places Bar. You can customize menu

options so you can place the functions you use most where they work best for you. You can also create and name custom menus and toolbars according to your needs. Custom menus and toolbars can include virtually any function that is available in PowerPoint.

If you want to keep your PowerPoint working environment uncluttered and display only the functions you use most, you can choose which toolbars appear when you open PowerPoint. You can also choose whether or not the Office Clipboard opens every time you copy data to it so that you can easily access copied or pasted items, or instead concentrate on your presentation by choosing not to view Clipboard contents automatically.

Quick Tips

You can view presentations in the format in which you are most comfortable when you change the default view in which presentations display. If you routinely change the way you view presentations in PowerPoint, you can save time by specifying the default view you would like PowerPoint to use instead of making

manual changes to the view each time you open a presentation. When you change the default view, PowerPoint displays only the parts of the screen that you want to see. After you specify the view you would like to use, you can see it take effect the next time you open a presentation.

① Click **Tools.**

② Click **Options.**

The Options dialog box opens.

③ Click the **View** tab.

④ Click the Default View ▼.

⑤ Click a view option.

⑥ Click OK.

The Options dialog box closes, and the next time a presentation is opened, the view is changed.

Did You Know?

You can always change a presentation's view after you open it. To view or remove the Notes Page, simply click View, and then click Notes Page.

Add a Shortcut to the My Places Bar

You can save time and access files quickly by adding a shortcut for commonly used folders to the My Places Bar. The My Places Bar appears on the Open and Save As dialog boxes and is most commonly used to access your Desktop, My Documents, My Computer, and My Network Places folders.

When you add a shortcut to the My Places Bar, it adds an icon to the bar that represents a file folder, network location, or even a Web site. When you want to open a file from that location, you can simply click the shortcut to see the list of files that are available.

ADD THE SHORTCUT

1. Click File.
2. Click Open.

The Open dialog box appears.

3. Click the Look in ▼.
4. Click a folder location.

5 Click the Tools ⬇.

6 Click Add to "My Places".

The shortcut is added to the My Places Bar.

USE THE SHORTCUT

1 In the Open or Save As dialog box, click the shortcut icon on the My Places Bar.

● The folder opens.

Did You Know?

Because all of the Microsoft Office 2003 programs use the My Places Bar, when you add a shortcut to your My Places Bar in PowerPoint, it is also accessible in other programs like Microsoft Word, Microsoft Excel, and more.

You can put the features you use within easy access by customizing menu bar options in PowerPoint 2003. You can easily add commands to menus or remove menu items that you do not need or use. You can move menu items that are currently nested in submenus to a place of higher prominence on the menu, or you

can easily rearrange menu items to put the tools you need where you need them. More advanced options allow you to change or add an icon next to a menu item, change the text label for a menu item, or even change the shortcut key for a menu item.

① Click Tools.

② Click Customize.

The Customize dialog box appears.

③ Click the Commands tab to customize your menus.

④ Click the Rearrange Commands button.

The Rearrange Commands dialog box appears.

⑤ Click the Menu Bar option (○ changes to ◉).

⑥ Click here and select a menu to edit.

⑦ Click Add.

The Add Command dialog box appears.

⑧ In the Categories section, click a menu from which you want to select a command.

⑨ In the Commands section, scroll down and click a command to add to the menu.

⑩ Click OK.

The menu is updated.

⑪ Click Close to close the Rearrange Commands dialog box.

⑫ Click Close to close the Customize dialog box.

The new command is added to the menu.

⑬ Click the menu to which you added a new command.

● The command is now visible on the menu.

Move It!
You can easily change the order of commands on menus. Follow steps **1** to 6 above. In the Controls section, scroll down and click the command you want to move, and then click the Move Up or Move Down button.

Create a New Menu

You can create your own menus to put all of the commands and tools that you need for a specific type of presentation in one familiar place. You can choose where to position your custom menu relative to the other menus.

Custom menus work well when you need to access tools that are normally found on different menus from the one you are using. For example, if you routinely work on presentations that require frequent edits to tables, additions of hyperlinks, and formatting of bulleted lists, you can easily set up a custom menu with a name you choose that you can use to link to these tools.

---

① Click Tools.

② Click Customize.

The Customize dialog box appears.

③ Click the Commands tab.

④ In the Categories section, scroll down and click New Menu.

⑤ Click and drag New Menu from the Commands scroll box to the position you desire on the menu.

● The New Menu item appears on the menu.

6 Click Modify Selection.

The Modify Selection menu appears.

7 Type a name for your menu in the Name field and then press Enter.

8 Click Close.

● The modified menu name appears on the menu.

Did You Know?

You can specify the shortcut key used to access a menu or menu item. Follow steps **1** to **7** above, but type an ampersand (&) before the letter you wish to use as the shortcut key in the Name box. For example, to make your custom menu named My Menu accessible when you press Alt+U, type My Men&u in the Name field. The menu will then appear as My Men<u>u</u>.

You can easily get to the tools you need by specifying which toolbars to display and which toolbars to hide by default when you open PowerPoint. Toolbars make it easy to find similar tools in one place display their contents in the user interface, making their features even faster to access. Unlike menus, you can reposition toolbars on the presentation on which you are working. You can also resize toolbars to expose all or only a few of the buttons contained in them. Toolbars take up screen space that you can use for editing your presentation; therefore, be selective about which toolbars you display.

① Click Tools.

② Click Customize.

The Customize dialog box opens.

③ Click the Toolbars tab.

4 In the Toolbars list, click the toolbars that you want to display (☐ changes to ☑).

5 Click Close.

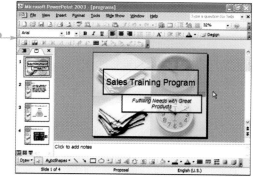

● The toolbars you selected appear.

Move It!

Each toolbar has four vertical dots (⫶) that help you move toolbars to a fixed position on the screen, such as any of the margins of the screen, or to floating positions on the screen where you can place them on top of the work area. To position a toolbar, click ⫶ on the toolbar that you want to move and then drag it to the desired position.

Turn On and Off the Office Clipboard

The Office Clipboard automatically saves up to 24 pieces of data that you copy. The Office Clipboard is a Microsoft Office resource that you can use across all Microsoft Office programs, including PowerPoint. The Office Clipboard provides a visual representation of the items stored, making it easier to collect information from a variety of sources and then selectively paste it. Data is automatically stored to the Office Clipboard when you copy data in Microsoft Office programs and Internet Explorer.

① Click View.

② Click Task Pane.

The Task Pane opens.

③ Click the Task Pane ▾.

④ Click Clipboard.

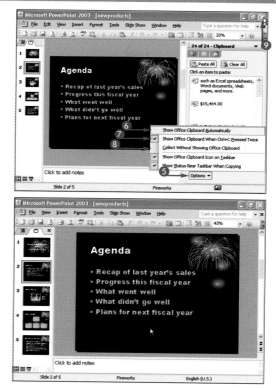

The Clipboard Task Pane appears.

⑤ Click Options.

⑥ Click to uncheck the Show Office Clipboard Automatically option (☑ changes to ☐).

⑦ Click the Show Office Clipboard When Ctrl+C Pressed Twice option (☐ changes to ☑).

⑧ Click to uncheck the Collect Without Showing Office Clipboard option (☑ changes to ☐).

⑨ Click ☒ to close the Clipboard Task Pane.

The Clipboard Task Pane closes.

The Clipboard still collects data, but the Clipboard does not open when new items are collected.

Try This!

If you are copying large amounts of data, such as large graphics files, they will stay on the Office Clipboard and in your computer's memory until you exit from all Office programs. To clear the Office Clipboard, follow steps **1** to **4** above, and then click the Clear All button on the Clipboard Task Pane.

Chapter 2

Give Your Presentation the Look You Want

You can use tools in PowerPoint 2003 to give your presentations a professional look that gets your work noticed. If you have ever wanted an easy way to check to see if your presentation meets visual goals, the Style Checker and the Office Assistant together can help. They can save you time by informing you when slides are becoming too cluttered or when too many fonts are being used. They can even suggest and then implement improvements for you.

You can also give your presentations a consistent format across presentations by using Slide Masters. You can create your own Slide Masters to suit your unique formatting needs.

You can emphasize a key message or logo when you place watermark text or a watermark image in the background of a printed slide. You can also place slide numbers on each slide in a presentation to make it easier for audience members to find particular slides.

If you are looking for ways to provide consistency across presentations, printed materials, and Web sites, you can find out how to change the fonts used throughout an entire presentation. You can use custom graphics or other materials from a Web site as bullets in your presentations or background images for slides. You can also quickly change the layout of slides whenever needed.

Quick Tips

Most instructors who teach presentation skills recommend guidelines for maintaining visual clarity, such as using font sizes that are large enough to be legible, limiting the number of bullets per slide, and limiting the number of lines per bullet. You can use PowerPoint's Visual

Clarity Rules to specify your own thresholds for font size, the number of bullets per slide, and the number of lines per bullet. Once these Visual Clarity goals are set, the Visual Clarity checker uses the Office Assistant to let you know when goals are not being met.

① **Click Tools.**

② **Click Options.**

The Options dialog box appears.

③ **Click the Spelling and Style tab.**

④ **Click the Check style option (☐ changes to ☑).**

If you do not have the Office Assistant enabled, a dialog box opens to prompt you to do so.

⑤ **Click Style Options.**

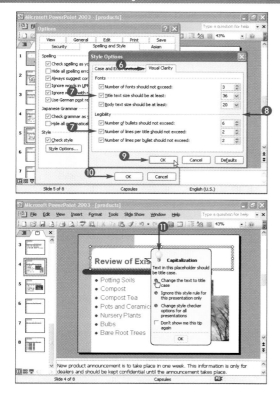

The Style Options dialog box appears.

⑥ Click the Visual Clarity tab.

⑦ In the Fonts section, click the Visual Clarity options you want to enforce.

⑧ Click here to specify the Visual Clarity settings you want for the items you checked in step **7**.

⑨ Click OK.

⑩ Click OK in the Options dialog box.

The Options dialog box closes.

The Office Assistant places a light bulb icon on each page that violates the Visual Clarity Rules you set.

⑪ Click each light bulb icon.

The Office Assistant suggests ways to change the presentation.

Attention!

You can see if the Office Assistant has been enabled on your computer by clicking Help and then clicking Show the Office Assistant. If it has not been installed, you are prompted to install it. You may have to go into the PowerPoint installation program to install the Office Assistant.

Slide Masters are templates that define how slides are formatted. Slide Masters also allow you to insert common elements on every slide, such as slide number, the date, footer text, or even logos or pictures. You may want to create a new Slide Master instead of editing the existing one if you want to apply it only to selected slides. You may also create a new Slide Master, and then apply it to the main Slide Master once you are sure how you want it. This task explains how to create a new Slide Master from an existing one, and then apply it to a slide or a presentation.

① Click View.

② Click Task Pane.

The Task Pane appears.

③ Click here and select Slide Design.

The Slide Design Task Pane appears.

④ Click View.

⑤ Click Master.

⑥ Click Slide Master.

The Slide Master View toolbar and the list of Slide and Title Masters appear.

⑦ Click Insert.

⑧ Click Duplicate Slide Master.

● The Slide Master and Title Master are duplicated. The new Slide Master appears in the Slide Design Task Pane.

⑨ Edit the new Slide Master as desired.

⑩ Click Close Master View.

The Normal View of your presentation appears.

⑪ Click the ▣ next to the new Slide Master.

⑫ Click Apply to Selected Slides.

The new Slide Master is applied to your slide.

Apply It!

You can apply the new Slide Master to all of the slides in your presentation. Follow steps **1** to **11** above, and then click Apply to All Slides.

Add a Watermark to Your Slides

Watermarks are commonly used to identify documents as a *draft*, as *confidential*, or with other messages. You can use watermarks to reinforce branding and corporate images by placing logos or marketing taglines behind text. Watermarks are most effective when they communicate the intended message without interfering with the slide. This is usually accomplished by using subtle

colors that maintain the legibility of slide content.

Watermarks are different from the graphics you insert into your presentation because they print behind your Notes or Handout pages. They also print on every page because they are placed on Notes or Handout Masters that duplicate the text or images to all pages.

① Click View.

② Click Master.

③ Click Notes Master.

The Notes Master appears.

④ Click View.

⑤ Click Toolbars.

⑥ Click Drawing.

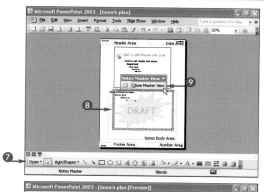

The Drawing toolbar appears.

⑦ Click to select a tool from the Drawing toolbar.

⑧ Click in the presentation and add a text box, an AutoShape, or a picture as your watermark.

⑨ Click Close Master View.

The Notes Master closes.

● When the Notes Page is printed, the watermark appears behind the text.

TIP

Did You Know?

You can also create watermarks behind Handout pages. Follow steps **1** and 2 above, and then click Handout Master instead of Notes Master.

Place Slide Numbers on All Slides

You may already be accustomed to placing page numbers on Slide, Handout, and Notes pages so that anyone following a printed copy of your presentation can easily find referenced pages. If an audience member wants to ask a question about a slide and there are multiple slides with similar titles, adding slide numbers makes it easier for a viewer to ask about a specific slide.

Slide numbers are included on Notes and Handout pages by default, but they are not turned on for slides by default. This task explains how to add numbers to all slides in a presentation, and then how to edit slide number formatting.

---

① **Click Insert.**

② **Click Slide Number.**

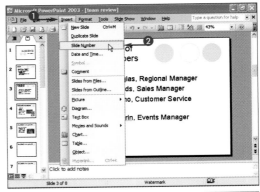

The Header and Footer dialog box appears.

③ Click the Slide number option (□ changes to ☑).

④ Click Apply to All.

The Header and Footer dialog box closes.

● The page number is applied to all pages in the format specified in the Slide Master.

⑤ Click View.

⑥ Click Master.

⑦ Click Slide Master.

The Slide Master View appears.

⑧ Click to highlight the slide number symbol (⟨#⟩).

⑨ Press Ctrl+B to change the font to bold.

You can also change the formatting of the slide number by clicking Format and selecting an option.

⑩ Click Close Master View.

Slide numbers are applied to all pages in the format specified.

Did You Know?

When you add slide numbers to the slides in your presentation, they are also displayed when you print your slides.

Changing all fonts at once can be especially useful when you have chosen to use a Design Template that has the look and feel you like, but uses a font that is different from what your company normally uses.

You can change fonts used throughout your presentation by changing the fonts in the Masters. However, changing fonts in Slide Masters does not affect text in items not controlled by the Masters, such as text boxes. If you want to change fonts throughout your presentation, including in Masters, text boxes, and more, you can use Replace Fonts.

① Click Format.

② Click Replace Fonts.

The Replace Font dialog box appears.

③ Click the Replace ✓.

④ Click the font you want to replace.

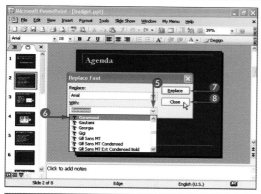

⑤ Click the With ▼.

⑥ Click the font with which you want to replace the existing font.

⑦ Click Replace.

⑧ Click Close.

The font is replaced throughout the entire presentation.

TIP

Caution!
Replace Fonts changes the font used everywhere in your presentation, including in Masters. Therefore, even if you select text that is 12-point Arial and use Replace Fonts to change it to Georgia, every instance of the Arial font will change to Georgia. Because the changes made with Replace Fonts are so global, use this tool with caution.

You can choose to emphasize slide titles by setting capitalization options for slide titles, such as sentence case, lowercase, uppercase, or title case. Sentence case capitalizes the first word of a line, lowercase uses all lowercase letters, uppercase capitalizes all letters, and title case capitalizes the first letter of each word.

You can use the Style Checker to set title capitalization rules, and you can choose to instruct the Office Assistant to alert you when a slide title does not meet the capitalization rules you set.

---

① Click Tools.

② Click Options.

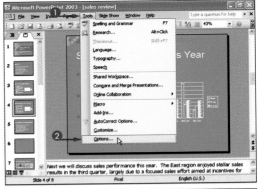

The Options dialog box appears.

③ Click the Spelling and Style tab.

④ Click the Check style option (☐ changes to ☑).

If you do not have the Office Assistant enabled, a dialog box opens to prompt you to do so.

⑤ Click Style Options.

The Style Options dialog box appears.

6 Click the Case and End Punctuation tab.

7 Click the Slide title style option (☐ changes to ☑).

8 Click here and select UPPERCASE.

9 Click OK to close the Style Options dialog box.

10 Click OK to close the Options dialog box.

The Office Assistant places a light bulb icon on each page that does not use uppercase titles.

11 Click each light bulb icon.

The Office Assistant suggests changes to the presentation.

12 Click the Change the text to upper case option to change the slide's title to all capital letters.

13 Click OK.

The slide title is capitalized.

TIP

Attention!

The Style Checker requires the Office Assistant. You can find out whether the Office Assistant has been enabled on your computer by clicking Help and then Show the Office Assistant. If it has not been installed, you are prompted to install it. You may have to go into the PowerPoint or Office installation program to install the Office Assistant.

Create Unique Points from Your Own Custom Graphics

You can use custom bullets that you create with a graphics program or utilize the bullets that you use on your Web site in your presentations as well. Using consistent graphics across all of the documents you create, as well as the presentations you produce, helps reinforce your company's brand and image with a unified look.

The graphics files from which you create bullets can be in any file format supported by PowerPoint, which includes virtually all of the most popular graphics files. Once you use a custom graphics file as a picture bullet, it continues to be accessible from the Picture Bullets library for other projects.

---

① Click and drag to select the text next to the bullets you want to change.

② Click Format.

③ Click Bullets and Numbering.

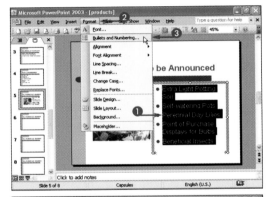

The Bullets and Numbering dialog box appears.

④ Click Picture.

The Picture Bullet dialog box appears.

⑤ Click Import.

The Add Clips to Organizer dialog box appears.

⑥ Click here to locate the folder where your graphic files are stored.

⑦ Click the name of the graphic file you want to use in place of the current bullet.

⑧ Click Add.

The Picture Bullet dialog box appears.

⑨ Click your custom bullet.

⑩ Click OK.

The Picture Bullet and Bullets and Numbering dialog boxes close.

● The presentation is updated with the new custom bullet.

Apply It!

You can easily change the bullets throughout your presentation by altering the bullets used in Slide Masters. To access Slide Masters, click View and then Slide Masters. Edit the bullets by following steps **1** to **10** above and then click Close Master View. All of the slides using that Master are updated with your custom bullets.

The Slide Layout Task Pane gives you a clear visual representation of the many available layouts so you can quickly identify the right layout for your content. You can use the Slide Layout Task Pane to apply a layout to a selected slide or to a new slide. Once the layout has been applied to the slide, you can easily insert pictures, text, audio, video, and more, and that content is placed according to your Slide Layout choices. If your content dictates a change in layout, you can easily choose from one of the other layouts whenever you want.

① **Click Format.**

② **Click Slide Layout.**

The Slide Layout Task Pane appears.

③ **In the Apply slide layout section, click the ▢ on the Slide Layout that you want to apply.**

④ **Click Apply to Selected Slides.**

The new slide layout is applied.

⑤ Click one of the icons to insert a table, a chart, a picture, a diagram, or a video clip.

The appropriate dialog box opens, for example, the Diagram Gallery.

⑥ Click the item you want to insert into the slide.

⑦ Click OK.

The item is inserted into the slide in the specified slide layout.

Apply It!

If the Slide Layout Task Pane is already visible and you want to create a new slide, follow steps **1** to **7**, but in step **4**, click Insert New Slide instead of Apply to Selected Slides.

Add Emphasis by Inserting a Custom Background Image

When you insert an image as a slide background, it does not print when the slides print. This is important, because if you apply a background image for its appearance, you do not want the image to conflict with the slide content. If you want the image to print with the slide, insert the image into the slide itself.

Background images are stretched or contracted to display on whatever screen that is being used. You will get better results if you use images that are approximately the same size as the monitor on which you will display them.

① Click Format.

② Click Background.

The Background dialog box appears.

③ Click the Colors ⊡.

④ Click Fill Effects.

The Fill Effects dialog box appears.

5 Click the Picture tab.

6 Click Select Picture.

Caution!

You will achieve the best results when you apply a background image that is 1⅓ times wider than it is high. The width of most computer screen resolutions is 1⅓ times the height, such as 800 pixels wide by 600 pixels high. Your background image should use these proportions as well. If the image you are using for a background is not in these proportions, the background image will look stretched or skewed when displayed.

continued

Pictures from digital cameras work well as background images for slides. Because most digital cameras create images with higher resolutions than are needed for use in presentations, you may want to reduce the size of the file in a graphics editing program. In addition to images taken from a digital camera, you can use

graphics files in any picture file format supported by Microsoft Office, including BMP, JPG, GIF, TIF, and more. Remember that if you use uncompressed files or files that are larger than needed, you may unnecessarily increase the file size of your presentation or even slow its performance when delivering a slide show.

The Select Picture dialog box appears.

⑦ Click here and locate the folder containing the file you want to use as the background image.

⑧ Click the file you want to use.

⑨ Click Insert.

The Fill Effects dialog box reappears displaying the image.

⑩ Click OK.

The Background dialog box reappears.

⑪ Click Apply.

The background image is applied to the slide.

Apply It!

You can also apply a background image to Notes Masters. To apply a background image to a Notes Master, click View, Master, and then Notes Master. Next, follow steps **1** to **11**. Use this option with caution because the notes text will print on top of the background image, which may affect legibility.

Add Impact
with Graphics

You can enhance the effectiveness of your presentations when you use graphics to help communicate your message. You can put content from your digital camera or scanner to work for you by inserting photos, drawings, and documents into your presentations. For example, if you have a printed photograph you would like to include on a slide, PowerPoint communicates directly with your scanner to scan the photograph and then insert it into your presentation.

Once your images or graphics are in your presentations, you can learn how to add effects to get them noticed. You can add colorful borders to make them stand out,

and you can crop photos so that only the most important parts are included in your slides.

If you have ever wondered how to make an image with a white background blend in on a slide with a color background, you can use the Set Transparent Color tool to make it work.

You can create a Photo Album that displays a collection of images or photographs in one of many available styles. Photo Album presentations are professionally formatted and save you time because, after selecting which images to include, all of the work of preparing the presentation is done for you.

Quick Tips

Digital cameras are popular because the images they produce have improved to near-photo quality in even inexpensive models. The digital images they produce are easy to use in PowerPoint presentations. You can use the software programs that come with most digital cameras to upload images from the camera to your computer's hard drive.

The images are stored on your hard drive in a graphics file format, such as JPG or GIF, which are supported by most graphics editing programs. You can crop images, resize them, add text, and more. Because PowerPoint supports these file formats, you can easily insert the images into your presentations.

① Click Insert.

② Click Picture.

③ Click From File.

The Insert Picture dialog box appears.

④ Click here and select the folder where your image is located.

⑤ Click the image you want to insert.

⑥ Click Insert.

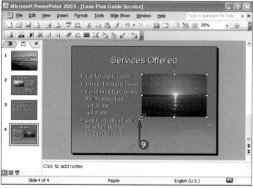

The image is inserted into the page at its original size.

7 Click the image to select it.

When you click the image, the image resizing handles become visible.

8 Click any corner of the image and drag it diagonally toward the opposite corner of the image to resize it.

9 Click and drag the image to the desired location on the slide.

The image is positioned on the slide.

Caution!

Digital cameras store images for printing at a quality higher than you need for presentations that will be viewed online. Higher-quality images result in larger file sizes; therefore, to keep your presentation loading quickly, you should compress your images whenever possible.

You can turn hard-copy photographs and other documents into digital images by using a scanner. Scanners convert documents, photographs, or other materials into electronic files. After the documents are scanned, they are usually stored as graphics files in formats such as TIF, JPG, and GIF.

PowerPoint combines the scanning of documents and inserting them into your presentations into an easy process. PowerPoint communicates with the scanner's software, which then communicates with the scanner to create the image. After creating the image, the software passes the image to PowerPoint to be inserted into the presentation.

① Click Insert.

② Click Picture.

③ Click From Scanner or Camera.

The Insert Picture from Scanner or Camera dialog box appears.

④ Click here and select the scanner you want to use to scan the image.

⑤ Click Insert.

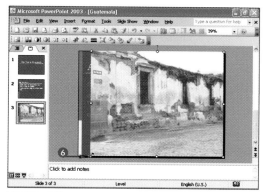

The scanner scans the image and then inserts it into the slide.

6 Click any corner of the image and drag it diagonally toward the opposite corner to resize it.

7 Click and drag the image to the desired location on the slide.

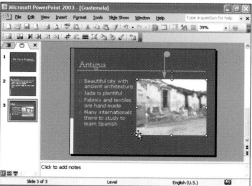

● The scanned image is positioned on the slide.

Caution!

Images are scanned using the scanner's default settings. Change the scanner properties before scanning if the image area is too large or too small, or the color or clarity of the image is less than desired. Follow steps **1** to **4**, and then click Custom Insert. Your scanner's property settings dialog box appears. Follow the scanning procedures for your scanner, and then follow steps **6** and **7** above.

You can use image borders to highlight items that users can click for some other effect. Traditionally, items you can click on a Web site have a colorful highlighted border around them. If you add a hyperlink to an image in PowerPoint, borders are not added automatically. You can go in and add borders to images that use effects like hyperlinks. Image borders in PowerPoint are simply lines placed around images. The true power in image borders is the ability to use virtually any color or any line width to make your image borders truly unique.

① Right-click the image.

The Edit menu appears.

② Click Format Picture.

The Format Picture dialog box appears.

③ Click the Colors and Lines tab.

④ Click the ⌄ Color .

⑤ Click the color you want to use for the border in the Color area.

⑥ Click the Weight ⬦ to set the line weight.

⑦ Click OK.

The image is updated with the new border.

Did You Know?

Line weights are measured in points. A point is equivalent to ¹⁄₇₂ of an inch. A line that is 12 pixels high is 12 dots high, or the height of a capital letter I in a 12-point font.

Cropping is especially useful if you routinely add digital camera images to slides. Digital images are often sized at a ratio of 1:1.5. For example, an image that is 4" high will be 6" wide, or 4" x 6". If you want to display the image as a square, you can crop to reduce the width. You can crop almost any type of image, except for animated GIF files.

① Click the image you want to crop.

② Click View.

③ Click Toolbars.

④ Click Picture.

The Picture toolbar appears.

⑤ Click the Crop button on the Picture toolbar.

The cropping handles appear on the picture.

⑥ Click one of the cropping handles, and then drag toward the center of the picture.

Repeat step 6 for each side or corner you want to crop.

⑦ Click the Crop button on the Picture toolbar.

The image is cropped.

Did You Know?

After you crop an image it will appear smaller, but it will not take up less space in your presentation until you compress it.

Graphics should be compressed after they are manipulated in PowerPoint. If your presentation is likely to be viewed on monitors rather than printed, you can compress the images for Web or screen resolution.

Even if you expect to print your presentations with high quality, you should compress graphics if they have been resized or cropped. When you resize or crop images, the visual image of the graphics file changes, but the actual size of the file remains unchanged. The Compress Pictures tool removes cropped or resized portions of images from files and decreases the file size.

① Click View.

② Click Toolbars.

③ Click Picture.

The Picture toolbar appears.

④ Click the image to compress.

⑤ Click the Compress Pictures button on the Picture toolbar.

The Compress Pictures dialog box appears.

6 In the Change resolution section, click the Web/Screen option (○ changes to ◉).

7 In the Options section, click the Compress pictures option (☐ changes to ☑).

8 In the Options section, click the Delete cropped areas of pictures option (☐ changes to ☑).

9 Click OK.

The Compress Pictures warning appears.

10 Click Apply.

The image is compressed.

Did You Know?

You can choose to maintain the screen resolution of existing images that you compress after they have been resized or cropped. Follow steps **1** to **10** above, but in step 6 make sure that the No Change option is selected (○ changes to ◉).

The Photo Album tool saves time because it allows you to insert many images at once and then formats the slides with the selected number of pictures. For example, without the Photo Album tool, if you wanted to arrange six images on two slides, you would have to create the slides, insert the images into the presentation, and then you would have to resize and reposition the images on the two slides. The Photo Album tool performs these tasks for you and applies selected special effects to the images, such as corner tabs or special shapes.

1. Click Insert.
2. Click Picture.
3. Click New Photo Album.

The Photo Album dialog box appears.

4. Click File/Disk.

The Insert New Pictures dialog box appears.

⑤ Click here, and select the file folder where your image is located.

⑥ Click the file you want to insert into your photo album.

Note: *You can Ctrl+Click to select more than one file at a time.*

⑦ Click Insert.

⑧ Repeat steps **4** to **7** if you want to insert more images.

The Insert New Pictures dialog box disappears.

⑨ Click here and select the Picture layout you want to use.

⑩ Click here and select the Frame shape that you want to use.

⑪ Click Create.

A new presentation is created with the photos displayed in a photo album style.

Did You Know?

You can copy slides created with the Photo Album tool into an existing presentation. However, you lose the ability to edit the pages that have been copied.

The Set Transparent Color option is helpful if you are placing an image onto a slide that is not rectangular and has a background color different from the background color used in your slide. Images that do not have irregular edges, such as rectangles, are not usually good candidates for the Transparency option because they could easily be cropped.

The Set Transparent Color option works when you click in an area of the image that contains the single color that you want to become transparent. After you click the color that you want to make transparent, every instance of that color in the image is made transparent.

① Click View.

② Click Toolbars.

③ Click Picture.

The Picture toolbar appears.

④ Click the image.

⑤ Click the Set Transparent Color tool on the Picture toolbar.

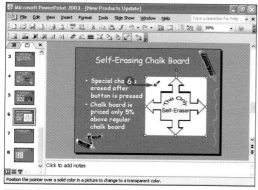

The ⌖ changes to a wand.

6 Click the color in the image that you want to become transparent.

The color you clicked is transparent.

Attention!

Many images, especially photographs, appear to have a uniform background color, when in reality there are slight variations in color. When the Set Transparent Color option is used on these images, not all of the background is made transparent.

Use Timesaving Tools

You can accomplish work faster in PowerPoint with tools that can help make routine work less tedious. For example, if you have ever become tired of retyping the same names or phrases repeatedly, you can use AutoCorrect to replace abbreviations with complete phrases, titles, or names. You can also reduce errors by instructing PowerPoint to fix the most common typographical errors automatically as you type.

You can eliminate guesswork by using the Format Painter to copy text and graphics effects from one place to another in your presentation. You can even turn one of your favorite presentations into a Design Template that you can use to create future presentations.

If you go to a Web site to do research and then become distracted by all of the options available online, PowerPoint's Research Task Pane helps you stay focused and on task. Its Internet search capabilities reduce distractions and bring you the tools you need where you need them. You can even use the Research Pane to look up words or phrases in the online dictionary or thesaurus, or translate words from language to language.

If you have ever wondered if there is a faster way to perform repetitive tasks, macros can help. The Macro Recorder in PowerPoint allows you to easily convert mouse clicks and keystrokes into Visual Basic for Applications code to help automate tasks.

Quick Tips

The Slide Sorter View and the slide tab on the Normal View are the most convenient places to copy slides because the thumbnail images allow you to select and then copy more than one slide at a time. When you copy slides from one presentation to another, by default, the copied slides take on the formatting of the new presentation. You can also choose to maintain the existing format of the copied slides.

① Click to select the slides you want to copy.

Note: *You can press Ctrl+click to select more than one slide.*

② Click the Copy button.

You can also press Ctrl+C to copy the slides to the Clipboard.

③ Click Window.

④ Click the presentation to which you want to copy the slides.

The presentation where you want to insert the slides appears.

⑤ Click where you want to insert the slides.

⑥ Click the Paste button.

You can also press Ctrl+V to paste the slides.

The slides are pasted into the presentation. The Paste Options Smart Tag appears.

⑦ Click the Paste Options ⏷.

The Paste Options are displayed.

⑧ Click the Keep Source Formatting option (○ changes to ⊙).

The slides return to their source format.

Did You Know?

You can paste slides from the Office Clipboard by clicking View, Task Pane, and then the Task Pane ⏷. Click Clipboard, and the Office Clipboard opens. Click where you would like to insert the slides in Slide Sorter or Slide tab in Normal View; then click the ⏷ on the Office Clipboard next to the slides you would like to paste. Click Paste.

You can reduce errors by letting PowerPoint automatically correct common typing mistakes. AutoCorrect maintains a list of mistyped words, as well as a list of the correct words used to replace them. When a word on the Replace list is typed and then a space or end punctuation mark is typed, the word is automatically replaced with the correct word from the Replace With list.

You can also use AutoCorrect to save time by adding abbreviations for commonly used titles, names, and phrases to the Replace list, and then specifying the longer text with which to replace them. You can also use AutoCorrect to correctly capitalize words or phrases.

① Click where you want to insert the AutoCorrect text.

② Click Tools.

③ Click AutoCorrect Options.

The AutoCorrect dialog box appears.

④ Type your AutoCorrect shortcut in the Replace field.

⑤ Type the text you want to replace the AutoCorrect shortcut when typed in the With field.

⑥ Click Add.

⑦ Click OK.

The AutoCorrect dialog box closes.

8 Type the AutoCorrect shortcut, and then press the spacebar.

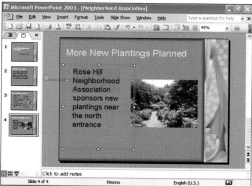

● The AutoCorrect shortcut is replaced with the AutoCorrect text.

Did You Know?

You can specify exceptions to the list of words to automatically correct. For example, you can specify not to automatically capitalize words that follow an abbreviation. This would prevent a phrase as *It is 6 ft. high* from being changed to *It is 6 ft. High* because of the period following the abbreviation. To add exceptions, follow steps **1** to **3** above, and then click Exceptions on the AutoCorrect dialog box. After you have specified exceptions, continue with steps **4** to **8** above.

The Format Painter is a tool on the Formatting toolbar that allows you to click one piece of text, copy the formatting of that text, and then apply that formatting to another piece of text. The Format Painter does not copy the text, just the formatting of the text. The Format Painter is especially useful when

you open a presentation that you did not create, and you are unfamiliar with the fonts, font styles, and other formatting used. For example, if some text in your presentation uses a custom color, you save time by simply using the Format Painter to copy the formatting and apply it to your presentation.

---

① Click the text from which you want to copy the format.

② Click the Format Painter button on the Standard toolbar.

● The 🔓 changes to the 🖌.

③ Click the slide that contains the text to which you want to apply the copied format.

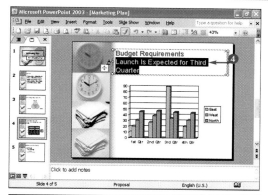

The slide opens.

④ Click and drag to highlight the text to which you want to apply the copied format.

● The format is copied from one area of text to another.

● The 🖌 changes back to ⬚.

Did You Know?

You can also use the Format Painter when you have an AutoShape in your presentation that has been formatted with colors, shadows, gradients, and other effects that could be difficult to identify and then reproduce on another AutoShape or image. You can follow the steps above to copy formatting from one image or AutoShape to another.

You can research Internet Web sites from within PowerPoint to save time and stay focused on your work. The Research Task Pane appears to the right of the PowerPoint work area so that you can continue to work on your presentations while you research.

You can also click and drag the Research Task Pane to other positions on the

screen, including floating on top of the work area. When you use the Research Task Pane, search results are displayed within the Task Pane. The Research Task Pane is preconfigured to search popular online reference books, research sites, business and financial sites, and sites you add to the list.

① Click View.

② Click Task Pane.

The Task Pane appears.

③ Click the Task Pane ▼.

④ Click Research.

The Research Task Pane appears.

⑤ Click the Research Options ⊡.

⑥ Click the Research Option you want to use.

⑦ Type the term you want to search for in the Search for field.

⑧ Click ➔.

Search results are displayed in the Research Task Pane.

Did You Know?

You can add or remove Web sites from the list of reference options in the Research Task Pane. Click the Research options link on the Research Task Pane, and then make sure that there is a checkmark (☑) next to each option you want to use. To add a site, click the Add Services button on the Research Options dialog box. Type the Web site address of the site you want to add in the Address field, click Add, and then click OK.

You can look for words by selecting Encarta Dictionary in the list of research options in the Research Task Pane. When you submit a word, the word's definitions and pronunciations are listed in the Task Pane with a list of alternative research options. The research portion of the Research Task Pane works much like an Internet browser.

You can also choose to find words in the online Thesaurus, which provides you a list of words that are similar in meaning to the ones you are researching. You can access the Thesaurus in the All Reference Books portion of the research options list in the Research Task Pane.

① Click View.

② Click Task Pane.

The Task Pane appears.

③ Click the Task Pane ▼.

④ Click Research.

The Research Task Pane appears.

⑤ Click the Research Options ☑.

⑥ Click the Encarta Dictionary option.

⑦ Type the word you want to look up in the Search for field.

⑧ Click 🡒.

Search results appear in the Research Task Pane.

Did You Know?

More online dictionaries are available on the Internet. To add one to the list of available reference services, click the Research options button on the Research Task Pane. Click the Add Services button on the Research Options dialog box, type the address of the Web site you want to add in the Address field, click Add, and then click OK.

You can translate words from one language to another by using the Research Task Pane. The Research Task Pane enables you to see translation results in various forms, such as nouns, verbs, or adjectives. The next time you select the Translation option on the Research Task Pane, the languages chosen on the last search are presented again, making it unnecessary to repeat language selections.

The Research Task Pane also displays additional fee-based options for translation services. You can use the built-in translation tool for translating a few words. For longer documents, however, machine or human translation services can be more accurate.

① Click View.

② Click Task Pane.

The Task Pane appears.

③ Click the Task Pane down arrow.

④ Click Research.

The Research Task Pane appears.

⑤ Click the Research Options ☑.

⑥ Click the Translation option.

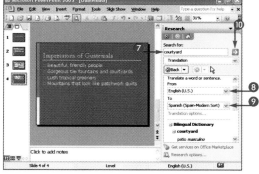

⑦ Type the word you want to translate in the Search for field.

⑧ Click the From ☑ and select the language from which you want to translate the word.

⑨ Click the To ☑ and select the language to which you want to translate the word.

⑩ Click ➡.

Search results are displayed in the Research Task Pane.

Caution!
You may be prompted to install translation services if you have not done so already. If prompted, click Yes to install the services. For example, the first time you use the Research Task Pane to translate a word from Spanish to German, you may be prompted to install the service. Afterward, the Bilingual Dictionary is accessible.

Custom Design Templates are especially useful if you have spent time customizing a presentation with the background colors, images, fonts, formatting, and graphics you like. Instead of copying and pasting an existing presentation, and then taking the time to replace all of the content, you can create a new Design Template and use as the foundation for a new presentation.

You can also create custom Design Templates that are variations of an existing Design Template. Instead of using the default Pixels Design Template and changing it each time, you can make your modifications once and make them forever available in the Slide Design Task Pane.

SAVE A PRESENTATION AS A CUSTOM DESIGN TEMPLATE

1. Click File.

2. Click Save As.

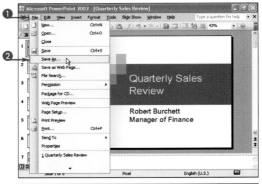

The Save As dialog box appears.

3. Click here and select Design Template.

4. Type the name of your custom Design Template in the File name field.

5. Click Save.

Your presentation is saved as a custom Design Template.

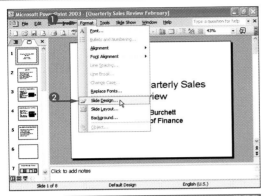

APPLY A CUSTOM DESIGN TEMPLATE TO A PRESENTATION

① Click Format.

② Click Slide Design.

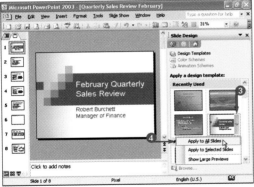

The Slide Design Task Pane appears.

③ Click ▮ next to your custom Design Template.

④ Click Apply to All Slides.

The custom Design Template is applied to all slides in your presentation.

Apply It!

You can choose to apply your custom Design Template to selected slides instead of all slides. Follow steps **1** to **3** to apply a custom Design Template to a presentation, but in step **4**, click Apply to Selected Slides instead of Apply to All Slides.

69

You can save time when you frequently repeat common operations by creating a macro. A macro contains one or more instructions that perform tasks you would normally do with your mouse or keyboard, such as clicking menu or toolbar options.

Macros are usually created to help speed up tasks with many steps or tasks that require clicking options on several menus. The Office Macro Recorder turns on when you create a macro and records your mouse clicks and keyboard operations. The Macro Recorder turns off when you click the Stop Macro button on the Stop Macro toolbar. When the macro runs, it performs the same tasks that were recorded.

① Click Tools.

② Click Macro.

③ Click Record New Macro.

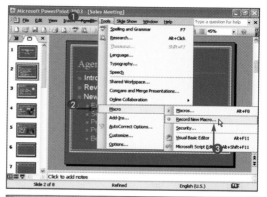

The Record Macro dialog box appears.

④ Type the name of your macro in the Macro name field.

⑤ Click OK.

The Stop Macro toolbar appears.

*Note: Steps **6** to **8** are the steps for recording a macro to change the view to gray. You may substitute the steps for the macro you want to record in steps **6** to **8**.*

6 Click View.

7 Click Color/Grayscale.

8 Click Grayscale.

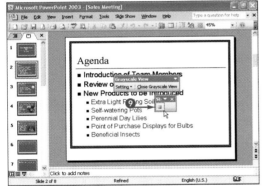

The screen changes to grayscale and the Grayscale View toolbar appears.

9 Click the Stop button on the Stop Macro toolbar.

The macro is recorded.

Caution!

The Macro Recorder records mouse clicks and keyboard operations, but does not record mouse movements. Therefore, you must perform some operations with the keyboard instead of the mouse in order to record properly. For example, you can highlight text by pressing F8 instead of using the mouse.

Run a Macro to Automate Your Functions

Macros are most commonly used to automate tasks that would otherwise require multiple steps or require accessing multiple menus or toolbars. Macros can greatly help save time and make working with programs like PowerPoint more efficient, but they have also proven to be a great way to spread computer viruses. You should enable and use macros only in presentations created by you or another trusted person, or programs that come from a company that has digitally signed it. Digital signatures come from certification authorities and allow you to find the vendor that produced a macro or program if there are virus or other security issues with it.

① Click Tools.

② Click Macro.

③ Click Macros.

The Macro dialog box appears.

④ Click the Macro in ⌄.

⑤ Click All open presentations.

⑥ Click the macro name in the Macro name field.

⑦ Click Run.

The macro runs, and, in this example, the picture is inserted, resized, and a border is placed around it.

Try This!

If you want to run a macro that is stored in the presentation you currently have open, follow steps **1** to **3** above; then click the macro name from the Macro Name field in the Macro dialog box. Proceed with step **7** to run the macro.

Add Sizzle to Your Presentation with Effects

You can use effects on your slides to create presentations that sizzle. You can apply a shadow effect to transform an image that blends into the background into something that appears to pop off the slide.

You can anticipate questions and prepare to answer them when you insert hyperlinks in text or images that link to other places in your presentation. You can even create a button that opens another program and another document when clicked.

You can create visually stunning presentations that use animation effects to add movement and interest. You can also add entrance or exit effects to text or graphics to help explain complex concepts

or illustrate relationships. For example, you can demonstrate sequences of events when you bring an AutoShape into a slide, explain it, and then click to remove the AutoShape and simultaneously replace it with another. In fact, you can choreograph multiple effects to occur on each slide just when and where you want them.

You can make your presentations look more professional by using transition effects to gracefully remove one slide and replace it with another. To enhance your presentation even more, you can apply one of the pre-built Animation Schemes to automatically apply transition, exit, entrance, and motion path effects to every slide in your presentation.

Quick Tips

Highlight Graphics with Custom Shadows

Shadow effects are colored duplicates of an object that are placed behind them to appear like shadows. Shadow effects give objects depth and often help differentiate them from their background. You can add shadow effects to images, AutoShapes, and even text. You can also choose to use

semitransparent shadows that allow the slide's background color to show through the top layer.

When your presentation uses a Design Template, default shadow colors are those used by the Design Template, giving the shadow effects a look that coordinates with the other elements in your presentation.

① Click View.

② Click Toolbars.

③ Click Drawing.

● The Drawing Toolbar appears.

④ Click the image or graphic to which you want to apply a shadow.

⑤ Click the Shadow Style button.

⑥ Click the shadow you want to use.

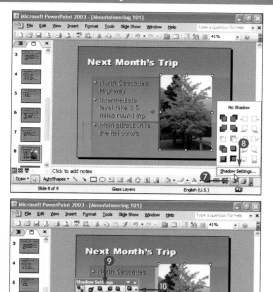

The default shadow is applied.

⑦ Click the Shadow Style button.

⑧ Click Shadow Settings.

The Shadow Settings dialog box appears.

⑨ Click the Nudge buttons to move the shadow up, down, left, or right.

⑩ Click the Shadow Color ⬛.

⑪ Click the color you want to use.

The color you select is applied.

Caution!
You should use care when you add semitransparent shadow effects. Because the background color shows through, sometimes results can be unexpected. For example, if your slide background color is yellow and you add a semitransparent blue shadow effect, it will appear as a green shadow. The yellow and blue blend together to yield green.

Create a Link to Go Elsewhere in the Presentation

You can quickly navigate to a specific slide in your presentation with a click of your mouse. Hyperlinks to different parts of your presentation work when you deliver your presentation in Slide Show Mode. By default, they appear on-screen as underlined text, and when you click them, the linked slide automatically appears.

Hyperlinks to other locations in your presentations can be particularly convenient when you anticipate questions at specific points in the presentation. You can click the hyperlink to quickly shift to the other slide to help answer those questions.

① Click and drag to highlight the text to which you want to add a hyperlink.

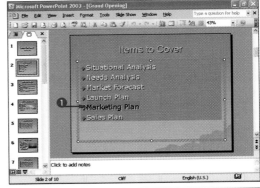

② Click Insert.

③ Click Hyperlink.

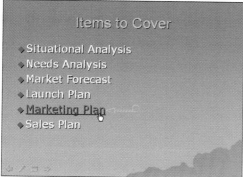

The Insert Hyperlink dialog box appears.

④ Click Place in This Document in the Link to section.

⑤ In the Select a place in this document section, scroll to locate the slide to which you want to link.

⑥ Click the slide.

● A preview of the slide appears in the Slide preview section.

⑦ Click OK.

The hyperlink is added to the slide.

⑧ Press F5 to display the slide in Slide Show Mode.

● You can click the active hyperlink to move throughout your document.

Did You Know?

You can link graphics and AutoShapes to other parts of your presentation. Click the object you want to link and then follow steps **2** to **8** above.

You can open a file in a separate program without leaving PowerPoint when you create an Action Button. Action Buttons are graphical buttons that you can draw onto a slide. You can assign actions to the buttons to perform key tasks. When you create an Action Button that opens a program, it allows you to stay in Slide Show Mode while the other program opens instead of exiting Slide Show Mode, minimizing PowerPoint, and then starting the other program. Action Buttons are convenient because you can create them from within PowerPoint; it is not necessary to use a separate graphics creation tool to create great-looking buttons.

① Click Slide Show.

② Click Action Buttons.

③ Click the Information action button
(➚ changes to +).

④ Click and drag to indicate a size for the action button.

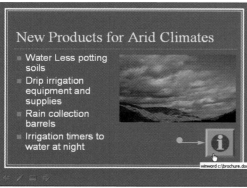

- When you release your mouse, the action button is drawn at the size specified and the Action Settings dialog box appears.

5 Click the Run program option (○ changes to ◉).

6 In the Run program field, type the shortcut for the program followed by the file path.

*For example, you could open a Word document called brochure.doc by typing winword **c:\brochure.doc** in the Run program field.*

7 Click OK.

The action button is created with a link to open the program and the specific document.

8 Press F5 to view the presentation in Slide Show Mode.

- You can click the button on the slide to open a document.

Did You Know?

You can open a different program. Find the path to the program by clicking Start and then All Programs. Right-click the program you want to locate and then click Properties. The path is listed in the Target field. You can copy it and paste it into the Run program field in step **6** above. Do not include the quotation marks.

Add Motion to Illustrate Your Content

Adding motion to graphics is a great way to focus attention on an important logo or graphic because the eye is naturally drawn to movement. It is also a good way to create effects like those produced with Macromedia Flash without using a separate tool or learning a separate program.

You can also apply more than one motion path to an image, each starting after you click your mouse. For example, you could have one part of a diagram slide into place, discuss it, and then click your mouse for the next part of the diagram to slide in, using the motion path you specified.

① Click Slide Show.

② Click Custom Animation.

The Custom Animation Task Pane appears.

③ Click Add Effect.

④ Click Motion Paths.

⑤ Click Draw Custom Path.

⑥ Click Curve.

The ⌖ changes to 🖼.

7️⃣ Click where you want the image to start and then click where you want the image to curve.

8️⃣ Repeat step **7** until the path is the desired shape.

9️⃣ Double-click at the end of the motion path.

● The motion path appears on the screen and the action is listed in the Custom Path section of the Custom Animation Task Pane.

🔟 Click here and select the speed you want to use.

⓫ Click Play.

The animation plays for you in the Custom Animation Task Pane.

Did You Know?

You can choose to start motion paths one after another instead of waiting for a click before the effect begins. After step **7** above, click the Start ▾ and select After Previous, then continue with step **9**.

Make an Entrance with Custom Animations

You can help illustrate important points better when you create builds out of graphics and text. *Builds* allow you to bring one element into a slide, discuss it, and then click when you are ready for the next element to enter. This is particularly useful when presenting diagrams that have multiple parts, each requiring explanation. One of the great parts about using builds is that it is not necessary to create a separate slide for each part of the build; all of the build elements make up a single slide. When printed, the slide looks like the results of all the builds.

① Click Slide Show.

② Click Custom Animation.

The Custom Animation Task Pane appears.

③ Click the item on which you want to apply the effect.

④ Click Add Effect.

⑤ Click Entrance.

⑥ Click Fly In.

The effect is added in the Custom Animation Task Pane.

7 Click here and select the speed at which you want the effect to occur.

8 Repeat steps **3** to **7** for each effect you want to add.

9 Click Play.

The animation plays for you.

Important!

It is usually easier to first create your slide with all text and graphics placed where desired, and then go back and create the build effects. This ensures that all of the slide elements fit together when the builds have completed.

Orchestrate an Exit with Custom Animations

You can use exit effects to generate excitement on slides. For example, you can use a combination of entrance and exit effects to display and then remove customer quotes or positive feedback to help give your slide visual impact and a feeling of excitement about the products or services being discussed.

By default, exit effects occur at high speed. However, you can set exit effects to take place more slowly for a more subtle style. You can create multiple exit effects on each slide, and after each build, you can preview your exit effects from within the Custom Animation Task Pane.

① Click Slide Show.

② Click Custom Animation.

The Custom Animation Task Pane appears.

③ Highlight the text on which you want to place an effect.

④ Click Add Effect.

⑤ Click Exit.

⑥ Click the effect you want to apply.

The effect is added in the Custom Animation Task Pane.

7 Click here and select the speed at which you want the effect to occur.

8 Repeat steps **3** to **7** for each effect you want to apply on the slide.

9 Click Play.

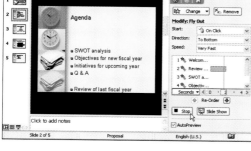

The animation plays for you.

Change It!

You can change the order in which exit effects take place. After following the steps above, click the effect you want to reorder, and then click the Re-Order ⬆ or ⬇ until the effect is in the desired order.

Choreographed effects can have different start or stop times and can include entrance effects, exit effects, motion paths, or even audio or video. When you want to discuss complex topics, choreographing effects can help you break them down into pieces that are easier to understand.

After each effect is created, it is listed in the Custom Animation Task Pane, where you can determine whether the effect begins with a mouse click or whether it begins after the previous effect is completed. This is useful when you want to illustrate how pieces fit together by displaying one piece, then another immediately thereafter. You can choose the speed at which effects occur.

① **Click Slide Show.**

② **Click Custom Animation.**

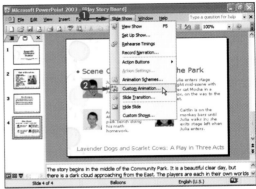

The Custom Animation Task Pane appears.

③ **Click the object on which you want to apply an entrance effect.**

④ **Click Add Effect.**

⑤ **Click Entrance.**

⑥ **Click the effect you want to apply.**

The effect is added to the object.

7 Click the object to which you want to add an exit effect.

8 Click Add Effect.

9 Click Exit.

10 Click the effect you want to apply.

The exit effect is added to the object.

11 Click here and select After Previous from the Start menu.

12 Click here and select a speed from the Speed menu.

13 Repeat steps **3** to **12** for each object on which you want to apply an effect.

14 Click Play.

The animation plays your arranged effects.

Did You Know?

If you have more than one element that you would like to enter or exit at the same time, you can group the elements first, and then apply the effect. Simply press Ctrl+click to select items such as text or graphics, and then follow the steps above.

Transition effects determine what happens between the time you click your mouse to advance to the next slide and the time the next slide loads. By default, presentations do not use transition effects. However, PowerPoint gives you many professional-looking transition effects you can apply to your slides. For example, the Dissolve effect removes blocks of your slide and then rebuilds it with the next slide.

When you apply a transition effect, you can see how it will look from within the Slide Transition Task Pane. Once you apply the transition effect to your slides, you can adjust the speed at which it occurs, and you can even include sound effects.

① Click Slide Show.

② Click Slide Transition.

The Slide Transition Task Pane appears.

③ In the Apply to selected slides section, click a transition effect.

A preview of the transition appears on the slide.

④ In the Apply to selected slides section, click the transition effect you want to use.

⑤ Click here and select the speed at which you want the transition to appear.

⑥ Click here and select the sound effect you want to play while the transition is occurring.

⑦ Click Apply to All Slides.

⑧ Click Slide Show.

The presentation plays in Slide Show Mode with the desired transitions.

Try This!

You can apply different transition effects to each slide. Simply omit step **7** above and then repeat the steps for each slide to which you want to apply a transition effect, omitting step **7** each time.

Add Interest with Animation Schemes

You can quickly and easily add movement to your slides by applying an Animation Scheme. Animation Schemes are preconfigured combinations of effects that you would normally have to apply individually. Animation Schemes can include entrance effects, exit effects, transition effects, motion paths, and more.

PowerPoint makes it easy to decide which Animation Scheme to use. You can view how the Animation Scheme will affect your slide from within the Slide Design Task Pane. Animation Schemes are also conveniently divided into three categories: Subtle, Moderate, and Exciting.

① Click Slide Show.

② Click Animation Schemes.

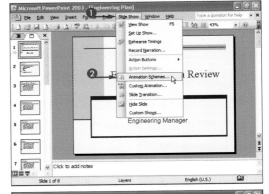

The Slide Design Task Pane appears.

③ In the Apply to selected slides section, scroll up or down to locate your scheme.

④ Click an animation scheme you want to apply to the slide.

● The effect is previewed on the slide.

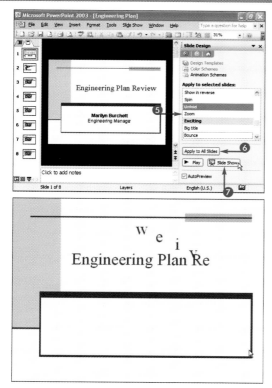

⑤ Repeat step **3** to experiment with different schemes before applying your selection.

⑥ Click Apply to All Slides.

⑦ Click Slide Show.

The presentation opens in Slide Show Mode with the Animation Scheme applied.

Did You Know?

When you use Animation Schemes, they often apply effects to bulleted lists that bring in a new bullet after each click. Trying to quickly advance to another slide in the presentation may mean a lot of clicking. To get to another slide faster while in Slide Show Mode, simply type the slide number and then press Enter.

Communicate with Audio and Video

You can enhance your presentations with audio and video to improve communication. Audio and video can come from a variety of sources, such as recordings from previous presentations, audio and video from the Clip Art Gallery, and even CDs.

You can play audio and video clips in a separate player, or you can embed the player into your slide so that the audio or video clip looks like it is part of the slide. Because Microsoft Windows Media Player comes with PowerPoint, it is the player used in this chapter.

The key to getting audio and video to play or record properly in PowerPoint is to first get the audio to play or record properly

outside PowerPoint. Once your audio/video capabilities are set up on your computer, you can use PowerPoint to record the audio for your presentation and automatically match that audio with each slide so that your viewers can listen to your audio at the same time they view your presentation.

If you want an audio or video clip to play only when you are ready for it, you can create a button that plays a clip when clicked. You can also play a sound when you hover your mouse over an object, or you can loop audio so it repeats indefinitely. You can also choreograph multiple sound or video effects on a slide to produce a professional presentation that gets your work noticed.

Quick Tips

You can add a button to your slide that, when clicked, plays a video clip. This is a great way to play video clips only when you are ready for them. The created button is an Action Button. Action Buttons make it easy to create a button of any size, and then assign an action to the button that takes place when the button is clicked.

In order to launch the player, you will need to know the name of the file that is executed to open that program or wmplayer.exe for Windows Media Player. You will also need to know the path to the file you want the player to open.

① Click Slide Show.

② Click Action Buttons.

③ Click Movie action button (⌖ changes to +).

④ Click and drag where you want to position the button.

Garden Tour Results

● The button is created, and the Action Settings dialog box appears.

❺ Click the Run program option (○ changes to ⊙).

❻ Type **mplayer2.exe** and a space, followed by the path to your video file, for example, **c:\gardentour.avi**, in the Run program field.

❼ Click OK.

The play video action is now assigned to the button.

❽ Press F5 to open the presentation in Slide Show Mode.

The presentation opens in Slide Show Mode.

❾ Click the video button.

The video plays.

Did You Know?

You can also browse to the program you want to open instead of typing the name. After step **5**, click Browse. On the Select a Program to Run dialog box, click the Look in 🔽, and then click the folder in which the program resides. Click the program, and then click OK. Then proceed with step **7**.

Video delivers more impact when it is integrated into your slide. For example, if your presentation is designed to train viewers on a particular topic, you can incorporate the Windows Media Player into your slide to allow them to see the video, stop it, adjust the volume, and more. You can also make the video more useful when you add a bulleted list of text to highlight key points.

When you insert the Windows Media Player Object into your slide, its properties are fully editable. You will need to know the path to the file to be played in order for the video to play successfully.

① Click Insert.

② Click Object.

The Insert Object dialog box appears.

③ Click the Create new option (◯ changes to ◉).

④ In the Object type section, scroll down and click Windows Media Player.

⑤ Click OK.

● The Windows Media Player control is inserted onto the slide.

6 Right-click the control to open the content menu.

7 Click Properties to open its dialog box.

8 In the URL field, type the path to your video file.

9 Click ⊠.

The Windows Media Player is configured to play your video file.

10 Press F5 to view your presentation in Slide Show Mode.

The presentation plays in Slide Show Mode with the video displaying in the Windows Media Player on the slide.

Did You Know?

The Windows Media Player Object does not automatically adjust its size to the size of your video, so it could be too small or too large for your content. You should know the dimensions of your video (height and width) in pixels and edit the Windows Media Player Object properties to match those dimensions. To do so, follow steps **1** to **8** above, and then type your video's width in the Width field and your video's height in the Height field. Then proceed with step **9**.

Add Sound from a File

You can make your presentations more interesting by adding audio clips. For example, if you are presenting a slide that discusses how happy customers are with your product, you can insert directly into the slide an audio clip of a customer talking about your product.

When you insert an audio clip from a file, a small audio icon is placed onto the slide. When you are ready for the audio clip to play while you are in Slide Show Mode, you simply click the audio icon and the audio plays. The audio clip does not play in an external media player; it plays through your computer's audio system.

① Click Insert.

② Click Movies and Sounds.

③ Click Sound from File.

The Insert Sound dialog box appears.

④ Click here and select the folder in which the audio file you want to play is located.

⑤ Click the file you want to play.

⑥ Click OK.

The Microsoft Office PowerPoint dialog box appears.

⑦ Click When Clicked.

The audio symbol is inserted into the slide.

⑧ Click and drag the audio symbol to where you want it to appear on the slide.

⑨ Press F5 to open the presentation in Slide Show Mode.

The presentation plays in Slide Show Mode.

⑩ Click the audio symbol.

The audio plays.

Did You Know?

You can choose to make your audio begin playing automatically instead of starting the audio with a mouse click. Follow the steps above, but in step **7**, click Automatically instead of When Clicked. However, with this option, you cannot click 🔳 to stop the audio when in Slide Show Mode.

Play On and On with Looped Audio

You can use looped audio to play music or a message repeatedly in your presentations. For example, if you plan to display a slide during a break in a conference, you may want to play music or an instructional message for the duration of the break. Adding a looped audio file to the slide will allow you to walk away from the presentation assured that the audio will continue to play until you return. After the audio clip is added to the slide, you can edit the Sound Object's properties to instruct the clip to play in a loop.

① Click Insert.

② Click Movies and Sounds.

③ Click Sound from File.

The Insert Sound dialog box appears.

④ Click here and select the folder in which the audio file is located.

⑤ Click the audio file you want to play.

⑥ Click OK.

The Microsoft Office PowerPoint dialog box appears.

⑦ Click Automatically.

A symbol representing your audio file ( ) appears on the slide.

⑧ Right-click the audio symbol.

The content menu appears.

⑨ Click Edit Sound Object.

The Sound Options dialog box appears.

⑩ Click the Loop until stopped option (□ changes to ☑).

⑪ Click OK.

The looped audio is set to play in your presentation.

Try This!
You can easily move by clicking and dragging it to the desired position on the slide.

You can enhance your presentation with audio directly from a CD. You can instruct PowerPoint to play audio directly from the CD player in your computer. For example, if you want to play music from a CD before and after a seminar, you can insert audio into introductory, and conclusion slides to play directly from a

CD. You can even specify exactly what tracks on the CD you want to play. The audio can be interrupted when you click to advance to the next slide.

When you deliver your presentation, a CD symbol is inserted into the slide that can be clicked to start playing the audio again from the beginning.

---

① Click Insert.

② Click Movies and Sounds.

③ Click Play CD Audio Track.

The Insert CD Audio dialog box appears.

④ In the Start at track section, click ☑ to select the track number at which you want to start.

⑤ In the End at track section, click ☑ to select the track number at which you want to end.

⑥ Click the Loop until stopped option (☐ changes to ☑).

⑦ Click OK.

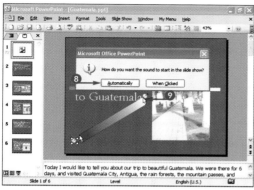

The Microsoft Office PowerPoint dialog box appears.

⑧ Click Automatically.

The CD audio symbol ( ) is inserted onto the slide.

⑨ Click and drag the CD audio symbol to where you want it on the slide.

⑩ Press F5 to view your presentation in Slide Show Mode.

The presentation opens in Slide Show Mode and the audio plays from CD.

Caution!
When you deliver your presentation, PowerPoint plays audio from whatever CD is in your computer's CD player. If you design your presentation with one CD in mind, but the CD player has another CD in it when you deliver your presentation, you could get unexpected results.

You can add depth to your presentations when you insert audio clips into your slides. You can make the effects look even more professional when you create buttons that link to audio clips. Placing a button on a slide with an audio symbol makes it obvious to presenters or viewers that supplemental audio is available.

Audio buttons are added to the slide by creating an Action Button, which is a professional-looking image that you can draw onto your slide in whatever size you want. They are called Action Buttons because you can assign actions that make them interactive, such as linking to an audio file when the button is clicked.

① Click Slide Show.

② Click Action Buttons.

③ Click the Sound action button (changes to +).

④ Click and drag where you want to position the button.

- The button is created, and the Action Settings dialog box appears.

5 Click the Run program option (○ changes to ⊙).

6 Type **mplayer2.exe** followed by the path to your video, for example, **c:\adspots.wma**, in the Run program field.

7 Click OK.

The play audio action is now assigned to the button.

8 Press F5 to open the presentation in Slide Show Mode.

The presentation opens in Slide Show Mode.

9 Click the audio button.

The audio plays.

Try This!

The easiest way to test and see whether an Action Button will work is to try typing the text in step **6** in the Windows Run dialog box. If it works from the Run dialog box, chances are that it will work from an Action Button. Click Start, Run, and then in the Run dialog box, type the code in step **6** in the Open field.

You can add entertainment value to text or images when you add an effect that plays a sound when you hover your mouse over the object. For example, if you have a slide presenting photos, you can add the sound of a camera.

You can add hover sounds to text or images by using Action Settings. Action

Settings allow you to create hyperlinks, run programs, run macros, or apply sound effects like Applause, Bomb, Camera, and Cash Register. You can also add more than one effect to an object, such as the launch of a video clip and a sound effect at the same time you hover over an object.

① Right-click the image to which you want to apply the hover effect.

The content menu appears.

② Click Action Settings.

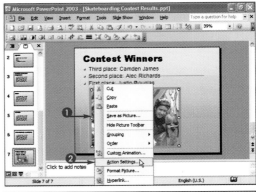

The Action Settings dialog box appears.

③ Click the Mouse Over tab.

4 Click the Play sound option (☐ changes to ☑).

5 Click here and select the sound you want to use.

6 Click OK.

The effect is applied to the image.

7 Press F5 to display the presentation in Slide Show Mode.

The presentation plays in Slide Show Mode.

8 Position your mouse cursor over the image.

The sound plays.

Contest Winners

⌐ Third place: Camden James
⌐ Second place: Alec Richards
⌐ First place: Justin Douglas

Did You Know?
You can also choose to apply audio effects to run when clicked instead of hovered over. Follow the steps above, but omit step **3**.

The Record Narration tool allows you to record audio for your presentation, and afterward, when the presentation is viewed in Slide Show Mode, your audio accompanies the slide.

When you choose to link narrations to a location on your hard drive, the audio file for each slide is stored separately on your computer. This keeps the file size down and keeps performance high. If you choose not to link narrations, the audio is stored with the presentation.

① Click Slide Show.

② Click Record Narration.

The Record Narration dialog box appears.

③ Click OK.

The presentation opens in Slide Show Mode.

④ Give your presentation while recording audio into your microphone.

⑤ Press the spacebar to advance to the next slide.

⑥ Repeat steps **4** and **5** for all of the slides to which you want to record narrations.

⑦ Press the Esc key when you have finished recording.

The Microsoft Office PowerPoint dialog box appears.

⑧ Click Save.

The presentation is shown in Slide Sorter View with the timings for each narration listed under each slide.

Change It!

Because each person's voice and volume varies, you will need to adjust most microphones to the correct levels before recording. PowerPoint includes tools to optimize recording. To access these tools, before step **3** above, click the Set Microphone Level button in the Record Narration dialog box.

You can go back and match audio clips with slides in a presentation that has been recorded. Once you match the audio clip with each slide, the audio clip plays automatically when the slide opens. For example, if one of your company's executives delivers a presentation at a conference where the audio is recorded,

you can package that presentation so that viewers can listen to the audio clip from the presentation at the same time they view the slides. In addition, you can hide the audio symbol when delivering the presentation in Slide Show Mode to keep your slides clean and uncluttered.

① Click Insert.

② Click Movies and Sounds.

③ Click Sound from File.

The Insert Sound dialog box appears.

④ Click here and select the folder in which the audio clip file is located.

⑤ Click the audio file you want to match to this slide.

⑥ Click OK.

The Microsoft Office PowerPoint dialog box appears.

⑦ Click Automatically.

The audio symbol (🔊) is inserted onto the slide.

⑧ Right-click the audio symbol.

The content menu appears.

⑨ Click Edit Sound Object.

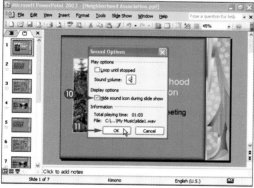

The Sound Options dialog box appears.

⑩ Click the Hide sound icon during slide show option (☐ changes to ☑).

⑪ Click OK.

⑫ Repeat steps **1** to **11** for each slide to which you want to add an audio clip.

TIP

Try This!
You can choose to play the audio when clicked instead of automatically. In step **7** above, click When Clicked instead of Automatically, and then proceed with step **8**. Omit step **10**, or you will not be able to see the audio symbol (🔊) on which to click.

You can use PowerPoint to produce a professional multimedia presentation. Multimedia presentations include audio, video, and effects. PowerPoint can help you synchronize all of them to play when and where you want.

You can use the Custom Animation Task Pane to reorder effects and change the speed at which they occur. You can also use the timeline to click and drag fields representing the beginning and end times for an effect to move them where you want in a graphical and easy-to-use fashion. Additionally, you can set effects to occur simultaneously with the previous effect, after the previous effect is finished, or upon clicking the mouse.

① Click Slide Show.

② Click Custom Animation.

The Custom Animation Task Pane appears.

③ Click an effect of which you want to change preferences.

④ Click here and select After Previous.

⑤ Click the Re-Order 🔼 or 🔽 until the effect is in the desired order.

⑥ Click an effect of which you want to change preferences.

⑦ Click here and select the speed.

⑧ Click the field that represents the effect you want to move, and then drag it to the desired position on the timeline.

⑨ Click the left or right margin of the field that represents the duration of an effect that you want to extend or contract, and then drag it to extend or contract the duration.

⑩ Click Slide Show.

The presentation plays in Slide Show Mode with the effects in the desired order and with the specified preferences.

Caution!
Because audio files have a fixed duration, you cannot click and drag the end point of an audio file displayed in the Custom Animation Task Pane to extend its play. Instead, you can loop the audio to make it repeat.

Enhance Your Presentations with Custom Content

You can communicate more effectively when you use specialized content to illustrate important information or concepts. You can include hyperlinks to Web pages in your presentations to bring in information and resources on demand to answer questions that arise. You can even include hyperlinks to e-mail addresses so that potential customers can easily reach you.

The Equation Editor can make fast work out of typing and formatting equations. You can also insert symbols to represent characters that are not on your keyboard, such as ®, ©, or even ™.

If you work with financial or statistical data, you can put it to good use by inserting it into your slide from a Microsoft Excel spreadsheet. You can even insert Excel functionality into your presentation if you want to display data that requires calculations. You can also graphically communicate numerical data in your slides by inserting an Excel-based chart.

You can use diagrams more effectively when you connect AutoShapes to form lines or arrows between objects. These lines stay connected even when you move the objects. You can also use the Organization Chart to update your organizational changes.

Quick Tips

Link to the Web from Your Presentations

You can create hyperlinks to pages or sites on the Web to supplement the content in your presentations. These links are available to click when you deliver your presentation in Slide Show Mode. When you click the link, your Internet browser opens with the Web page loaded.

You can also create hyperlinks to pages on your company's intranet site, as well as add hyperlinks to graphics, AutoShapes, or other objects on your slides. To create a hyperlink on a graphic or AutoShape, follow the steps below, but in step 1, click the graphic or AutoShape, and then proceed with step 2.

① **Highlight the text to which you want to add the hyperlink.**

② **Click Insert.**

③ **Click Hyperlink.**

The Insert Hyperlink
dialog box appears.

④ Click Existing File or Web
Page in the Link to
section.

⑤ Type the address for the
Web page you want to
link to in the Address
field.

⑥ Click OK.

The Insert Hyperlink
dialog box closes.

⑦ Press F5 to view the slide
in Slide Show Mode.

● The slide appears in
Slide Show Mode with
the hyperlink.

TIP

Change It!

By default, when you hover your mouse over the hyperlink, the target
URL appears. If you want it to display different text, follow steps **1** to
5 above, and then click the ScreenTip button. Type the desired text in
the ScreenTip text box in the Set Hyperlink ScreenTip dialog box, and
then click OK.

Add a Link to an E-mail Address

You can make it easy for customers or potential customers to reach you when you include hyperlinks to your e-mail address. When the presentation is in Slide Show Mode, the hyperlink is clickable.

When links to e-mail addresses are clicked, the viewer's default e-mail client is opened, a new e-mail message is created, and the message is preaddressed to the

e-mail address specified. When viewers finish with the e-mail message, they must return to PowerPoint to complete the presentation, so you might want to include links to e-mail addresses at the end of your presentation so you do not risk losing viewers before they are finished with the presentation.

① Highlight the text to which you want to insert a hyperlink.

② Click Insert.

③ Click Hyperlink.

The Insert Hyperlink dialog box appears.

④ Click E-mail Address.

⑤ In the E-mail address field, type the complete e-mail address of the message's intended recipient.

⑥ In the Subject field, type the subject of the message.

⑦ Click OK.

The Insert Hyperlink dialog box closes.

⑧ Press F5 to preview the slide in Slide Show Mode.

The presentation opens in Slide Show Mode with the hyperlink inserted onto the slide.

Picture of the Month!

• Be sure to send in your entry for next month's Picture of the Month!

Did You Know?

A hyperlink is also differentiated from normal text by its font color. If your presentation does not use a Design Template, hyperlinks are blue by default. If your presentation does use a Design Template, the Design Template determines the hyperlink font color.

Explain It Better with Equations

If presenting material that contains equations is part of your job, you know that creating and formatting equations can be cumbersome because they can include symbols, characters, and shapes that are not found on a standard keyboard. The Equation Editor is a program that comes with PowerPoint that eases the creation and editing of equations.

The Equation Editor is not included on any of the default toolbars or menus. You must add the Equation Editor to one of the toolbars so that you can easily access it in the future. After the Equation Editor button is visible on a toolbar, you can click it to open the Equation Editor.

① Click View.

② Click Toolbars.

③ Click Customize.

The Customize dialog box appears.

④ Click the Commands tab.

⑤ In the Categories section, click Insert.

⑥ In the Commands section, scroll down to Equation Editor.

⑦ Click and drag the Equation Editor onto one of the visible toolbars.

The Equation Editor button (√α̅) appears on the toolbar.

⑧ Click Close on the Customize dialog box.

The Customize dialog box closes.

9 Click the Equation Editor button.

The Equation Editor dialog box appears.

10 Type your equation.

11 Click File.

12 Click Exit and Return.

The equation appears in your slide.

Attention!
You may be prompted to install the Equation Editor after step **9** above. When prompted, click Yes to install it.

Type Specialized Characters and Symbols

You can type characters that are not available on your keyboard when you insert symbols into your slides. You can use symbols for business purposes to type special characters like copyright ©, registered trademark ®, or trademark ™. You can also use characters from foreign alphabets.

Each font has its own collection of symbols. If you use a specific font in your presentation, you may need to use a different font for the symbol you want to use. For example, if you use an Arial font in your presentation, but you want to insert a check box symbol (☑), you will find it in the Wingdings font.

---

① Click where you want to insert a symbol.

② Click Insert.

③ Click Symbol.

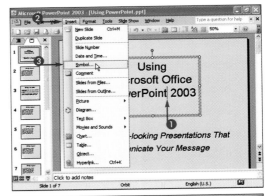

The Symbol dialog box appears.

④ Click here and select the font you want to use.

⑤ Click the symbol you want to insert into your slide.

⑥ Click Insert.

7 Click Close.

8 Repeat steps 1 to 7 for each symbol you want to insert into your slide.

● The symbols appear in your slide.

Caution!

When you insert a symbol, the Symbol dialog box remains open after the insertion. You can continue to insert symbols, but if you do, they will appear next to one another. If you do not want to have to reopen the Symbol dialog box each time you want to insert a symbol, you can insert all that you will need at one time and in one location, and then cut and paste them to the location desired.

Add an Excel Spreadsheet to Leverage Data

You can save time and reduce the need to retype data when you insert an Excel spreadsheet into your slide. When you insert an Excel spreadsheet into your presentation, the entire spreadsheet appears in its original format. When you click the object that represents that file, the menu options change to give you Excel functionality from directly within PowerPoint.

Because most Excel spreadsheets are not designed for presentation on a large screen, you will most likely want to adjust font sizes to make the data easier to read. You can do this by highlighting the text and using the standard tools in PowerPoint to increase the font size.

---

① Click Insert.

② Click Object.

The Insert Object dialog box appears.

③ Click the Create from file option (○ changes to ⊙).

④ Click Browse.

The Browse dialog box appears.

⑤ Click here and select the folder in which the spreadsheet is located.

⑥ Click the Excel spreadsheet you want to insert into the slide.

⑦ Click OK.

The Insert Object dialog box appears.

⑧ Click OK.

● The spreadsheet inserts into the slide.

Did You Know?

You can resize the spreadsheet object by clicking and dragging the object borders.

Add an Excel Spreadsheet to Calculate Data

If your slides routinely include information that requires calculations, you may be accustomed to using a calculator and then typing the results into a PowerPoint table. Instead, you can insert Excel spreadsheet capabilities directly into the slide so that the calculations take place where the data resides.

When you are not editing the spreadsheet, it appears as an object on the slide, and the menus return to standard PowerPoint menus. When you click the spreadsheet object to edit it, menu options are updated to reflect editing options.

① Click Insert.

② Click Object.

The Insert Object dialog box appears.

③ Click the Create new option (○ changes to ⊙).

④ In the Object type section, scroll down to locate the type of object you want to insert into your presentation.

⑤ Click Microsoft Office Excel Worksheet.

⑥ Click OK.

An empty spreadsheet appears in the slide.

7 Type your data and use formatting tools as in Excel.

8 Press F5 to view the presentation in Slide Show Mode.

The presentation opens in Slide Show Mode with the Excel spreadsheet appearing as a table.

TIP

Try This!

Once your data is entered into the Spreadsheet Object, you can use AutoFormat to give it a professional look. Highlight the area to which you want to apply the AutoFormat, click Format, and then AutoFormat. Click the AutoFormat style you want to use, and then click OK.

PowerPoint charts use Microsoft Excel chart tools, but you do not need to know how to use Excel to be successful in using charts. When you insert a chart into a slide, a sample chart is inserted with sample data opened in a datasheet for you to edit. You can type your data over the sample data, and as you do, the chart updates automatically.

The slide's Design Template determines the fonts that are used in the charts and the colors that are used on the bars to make your charts blend in with other elements in your slides.

① Click Insert.

② Click Chart.

A sample chart and associated datasheet are inserted into the slide.

③ Click inside the datasheet.

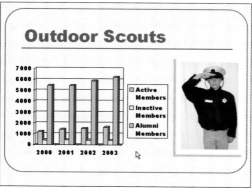

④ Type the data on which you want to base the chart.

The chart updates automatically with your new data.

⑤ Click ⊠ to close the datasheet.

⑥ Click the slide outside the chart area to exit from chart editing.

⑦ Press F5 to view the presentation in Slide Show Mode.

The presentation opens in Slide Show Mode and the slide contains your custom chart.

Change It!

You can change the default chart to any of the other chart styles, including Bar, Line, Pie, and more. Right-click the chart, click Chart Type, and then click the chart style in the Chart type section. Click OK, and the chart is changed.

Connectors are straight or curved lines or arrows that connect two or more drawing objects, such as AutoShapes, images, or other graphics. Connectors automatically anchor themselves to the midpoint of a side of an object.

For example, in a diagram that contains six boxes that illustrate key concepts, you can demonstrate relationships by drawing an arrow from one box to the next. If you move one of the boxes, the lines stay connected, making editing diagrams easier than ever.

① Click View.

② Click Toolbars.

③ Click Drawing.

The Drawing toolbar appears.

④ Click AutoShapes.

⑤ Click Connectors.

⑥ Click the connector you want to use.

When you hover over objects, a connection point displays on each side and corner, depending on the type of connector you select.

⑦ Click one of the connection points on the object from which you want to start the connector.

⑧ Click one of the connection points on the object to which you want to end the connector.

The connector appears between the shapes.

⑨ Repeat steps **4** to **8** for each connector desired.

The slide appears with the connectors.

Did You Know?

There are three types of connectors. Straight connectors use a straight line, Elbow connectors use straight lines and right angles, and Curved connectors use curved lines.

Show Relationships with Organization Charts

Organization Chart saves time because it not only creates a sample organization chart for you, it makes it easy to add or remove Subordinates, Coworkers, or Assistants at the appropriate levels in the organization. It also resizes the chart automatically as the number of represented employees grows. Changing the names on organization charts is easy because all you have to do is click the AutoShape and start typing. You can also rearrange team members on the organization chart by clicking and dragging their AutoShapes to the desired location.

① Click Insert.

② Click Diagram.

The Diagram Gallery dialog box appears.

③ Click Organization Chart.

④ Click OK.

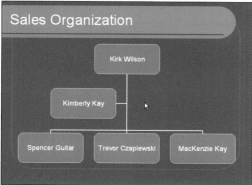

An organization chart is inserted into your slide.

⑤ Click one of the boxes and type a name.

⑥ Right-click a box.

The content menu appears.

⑦ Click the type of box you want to insert.

⑧ Repeat steps **5** to **7** to continue creating your organization chart.

⑨ Press F5 to view the slide in Slide Show Mode.

The presentation appears in Slide Show Mode with the organization chart in the slide.

Change It!

You can change the style of the organization chart. Click the box representing the highest-level manager, right-click the organization chart, and then click Show Organization Chart Toolbar. Click the Layout ☑, and then click the style you want to use.

Chapter 8

Expand Your Audience by Publishing to the Web

You can greatly expand your audience by publishing your presentations with Internet access. When you publish presentations to an intranet or Internet server, the presentations load as Web pages and are viewable even by those who do not have PowerPoint.

If you have access rights to a Web server, you can publish your presentation directly to the Internet, with no requirement for a separate Web publishing program. You can also use Web Page Preview to view how your presentation will look before you publish it to a Web site.

When a presentation is saved to the Web, the presentation's outline is used to create a list of hyperlinks to each slide to make it easy for viewers to navigate to the slides in your presentation. You can specify the colors, the fonts, and even the page title that appears at the top of the page to make the Web presentation your own. You can also specify the alternative text that appears while an image is loading on a Web-based presentation.

If you know the screen resolution at which viewers will have their monitors set, you can create your presentation to look custom-made for that screen resolution. You can even optimize your presentation to work best on a specific brand or version of browser.

Quick Tips

When you use Web Page Preview, PowerPoint creates an online presentation that displays in your browser. It creates the presentation in the Single File Web Page file format, ending with an .mhtml extension. Single File Web Pages allow you to distribute a single file that plays a series of Web pages. This is important

because Web-based presentations normally include many separate HTML files and a separate folder containing all of the graphics files. The Single File Web Page format allows you to see what viewers will see if you create and then give them a presentation in Single File Web Page format.

① **Click File.**

② **Click Web Page Preview.**

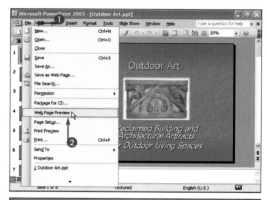

The presentation appears in the browser.

③ **Click the slide advancement right arrow to preview your presentation.**

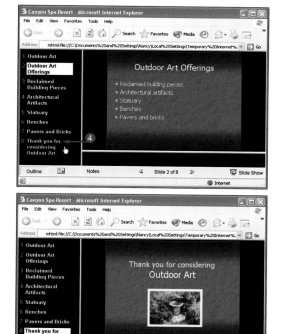

The presentation advances to the next slide.

④ Click one of the slides listed in the outline area to preview.

The presentation advances to the specific slide.

Caution!

Web Page Preview creates a temporary file on your computer. If you want to create an online presentation to use, follow the steps in the tip entitled "Turn Your Presentation into an Online Resource." Otherwise, the presentation is removed when you remove temporary files from your computer.

When you use the Save as Web Page option to create a Single File Web Page, you can post it on a file server, an intranet, or Internet Web server for anyone to access and view. Users can double-click the file from an e-mail message or network location to open their browser and load the presentation. When

users click a link to the presentation, they are prompted to open the presentation in their browser, or save it to their computer's hard drive. The ability to save the entire presentation to the hard drive makes Single File Web Pages an attractive way to distribute your presentations.

① Click File.

② Click Save as Web Page.

The Save As dialog box appears.

③ Click here and select the folder in which you want to save the online presentation.

④ Click Save.

The presentation is saved for use in a Web browser.

⑤ Open Windows Explorer.

Note: A fast way to open Windows Explorer is to click Start and Run, type **explorer.exe**, and then press Enter.

⑥ Click here and select the folder in which your browser-based presentation resides.

⑦ Double-click the file to open it.

The online presentation opens in the browser.

Did You Know?

You can create HTML pages instead of Single File Web Pages. The HTML option creates a single Web page for each slide. To save a presentation as HTML, follow steps **1** to **3** above, and then click the Save as type ⌄ and select Web Page. Proceed with step **4**. A folder is created that contains the HTML pages and a separate graphics folder.

Instead of creating Single File Web Pages or HTML pages for your presentation and then using a Web site publishing or FTP program to transfer the files to your Web server, you can use Save as Web Page. Save as Web Page allows you to specify a target server URL to which to publish, creates the necessary files, and then moves them to the Web server for you. Save as Web Page makes publishing to a Web server nearly as easy as saving a document. Once the presentation has been published to the Web server, it can be linked to any other Web page.

① Click File.

② Click Save as Web Page.

The Save As dialog box appears.

③ Click Publish.

The Publish as Web Page dialog box appears.

④ Type the path to the Web server and the target file name in the File name section.

⑤ Click the Open published Web page in browser option (☐ changes to ☑).

⑥ Click Publish.

Note: You may receive a prompt to enter a user name and password in order to access the site.

The presentation is published to the Web server, and the browser opens with the presentation loaded.

Caution!

You must have the proper security and permissions to access the Web server. A prompt will ask you to supply a valid user name and password before you can access the Web server.

As part of the publishing process, you can specify default fonts used in Web presentations. You can specify proportional fonts and fixed-width fonts. Proportional fonts allow each character to take up a different amount of space. For example, a letter i would be narrower than a letter w in a proportional font. Fixed-width fonts dedicate the same amount of space for every character. Most browsers specify the use of default proportional fonts and fixed-width fonts when fonts are not specified on Web pages, or when the specified fonts are not available. By specifying the default fonts for a Web-based presentation, you can override your selected defaults.

① Click File.

② Click Save as Web Page.

The Save As dialog box appears.

③ Click Publish.

The Publish as Web Page dialog box appears.

④ Click Web Options.

The Web Options dialog box appears.

⑤ Click the Fonts tab.

⑥ Click here and select the proportional font you want to use.

⑦ Click here and select the fixed-width font you want to use.

⑧ Click OK.

The Web Options dialog box closes.

⑨ To continue publishing, follow steps **3** to **6** in the task entitled "Publish Your Presentation Directly to a Web Site."

The presentation is published using the fonts you specified.

Did You Know?
You can specify the default proportional font size. Follow steps **1** to **6** above, and then click the Size ☑ to select the default proportional font size.

Customize Colors in Web-Based Presentations

By default, the Outline and Notes panes in online presentations have a black background with white fonts. However, you can publish your presentations using colors that coordinate with your presentation's look and feel instead of using the default black.

You can change Web presentation colors during the publishing process. When you choose to use the Presentation colors (font color) option, PowerPoint uses the default colors and primary font color from the design template applied to your presentation. For example, if you use the Glass Layers Design Template in green, you may want the Outline, Notes, and Presentation panes to use the same green background as well.

---

① Click File.

② Click Save as Web Page.

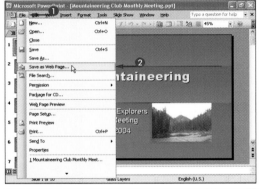

The Save As dialog box appears.

③ Click Publish.

The Publish as Web Page dialog box appears.

④ Click Web Options.

The Web Options dialog box appears.

⑤ Click the General tab.

⑥ Click the Add slide navigation controls option (☐ changes to ☑).

⑦ Click here and select the color option you want to use.

⑧ Click OK.

⑨ To continue publishing, follow steps **3** to **6** in the task entitled "Publish Your Presentation Directly to a Web Site."

The presentation is published with Web interface using your color selections.

Caution!

You can change the default background color to the default background color of the viewer's browser. Simply follow the steps above, but in step **7** click Browser colors instead of Presentation colors (text color). However, results will be unpredictable.

Change the Title for a Web-Based Presentation

You can change text that appears at the top of a viewer's Web browser when you create online presentations by changing the title bar text. The title bar appears at the top left of the browser window, and helps users identify the page that they are viewing.

Page titles can draw attention to important messages. For example, if your presentation is promoting a new product or service, you can include special characters, such as !, *, or #, in the page title to draw attention to it. Because this information appears in the user's browser, it is another good way to communicate a message to viewers.

① Click File.

② Click Save as Web Page.

The Save As dialog box appears.

③ Click Change Title.

The Set Page Title dialog box appears.

④ Type the page title in the Page title field.

⑤ Click OK.

The Set Page Title dialog box closes.

⑥ To continue publishing, follow steps **3** to **6** in the task entitled "Publish Your Presentation Directly to a Web Site."

● The presentation is published with the specified title on the browser title bar.

Did You Know?

Page titles are also used when viewers switch from program to program by pressing Alt+Tab. Text length is limited in the program switching dialog box, so you should make sure that page titles are not too long.

You can make images more meaningful in online presentations for users on slow Internet connections by setting alternative text for images. Alternative text instructs browsers to display text while images are loading or when images cannot be displayed.

Users with slow Internet connections often set their browsers to not display images. That allows them to quickly bring up Web pages because images are often the biggest elements to download. If you do not specify text that should appear in place of images, the user sees only an icon explaining that an image is missing. If you specify alternative text, the viewer sees the specified text in place of the image.

① Right-click the picture to which you want to assign alternative text.

The content menu appears.

② Click Format Picture.

The Format Picture dialog box appears.

③ Click the Web tab.

④ In the Alternative text box, type the alternative text.

⑤ Click OK to close the dialog box.

The alternative text is assigned to the image.

6 Click File.

7 Click Web Page Preview.

● The alternative text displays while the image loads.

Caution!

Alternative text can be as long as you want, but not all browsers will display all of the text. Therefore, it is a good idea to keep alternative text relatively brief.

Change the Target Screen Resolution for Web-Based Presentations

When you publish your presentation online, it is often difficult to anticipate the size at which viewers will have their screens set. One user may have an older monitor that is set at a smaller size of 640 pixels wide by 480 pixels high. Another may have a newer, larger monitor that is set at 1024 x 768.

When you know that users have newer monitors, you can predict that most will view presentations at 800 x 600 or 1024 x 768. You can also set the screen resolution to work best on smaller screens. For example, a presentation for a sales force using handheld devices could be optimized for 544 x 376.

① Click File.

② Click Save as Web Page.

The Save As dialog box appears.

③ Click Publish.

The Publish as Web Page dialog box appears.

④ Click Web Options.

The Web Options dialog box appears.

⑤ Click the Pictures tab.

⑥ Click the Screen size ⌄.

⑦ Click the desired screen size.

⑧ Click OK.

The target screen size is set, and the presentation is published optimized at the specified screen resolution.

⑨ To continue publishing, follow steps **3** to **6** in the task entitled "Publish Your Presentation Directly to a Web Site."

Include It!

You can optimize the screen resolution when you want to display the content of a frame in another browser window. For example, if you publish at a smaller screen resolution, you can bring the presentation into another Web page and still have room for additional content.

Optimize Your Presentation for a Specific Browser

You can help assure that your online presentation is accessible by users with the most popular browsers when you optimize your presentation for specific browsers. Options include Microsoft Internet Explorer 3.0 or later and Netscape Navigator 3.0 or later. Default Web presentations are optimized for Microsoft Internet Explorer 4.0 or later

because the majority of Internet browsers used fall in this category. If you are creating a Web presentation for use on the Internet, you may want to optimize your presentation for Internet Explorer 3.0 and Netscape Navigator 3.0 or later to make your presentation viewable by a broad array of users with a variety of Web browsers.

① Click File.

② Click Save as Web Page.

The Save As dialog box appears.

③ Click Publish.

The Publish as Web Page dialog box appears.

④ Click Web Options.

The Web Options dialog box appears.

⑤ Click the Browsers tab.

⑥ Click the People who view this Web page will be using ⌄.

⑦ Click the browser or browser combination you want to target.

⑧ Click OK.

The presentation is published optimized for the chosen browser or browser combination.

⑨ To continue publishing, follow steps 3 to 6 in the task entitled "Publish Your Presentation Directly to a Web Site."

Caution!

Online presentation files get larger as more browser brands and versions are supported because additional code is necessary to support features in older browsers. Be conservative in the range of browsers for which you choose to optimize your presentation. Optimizing your presentation for Internet Explorer 6.0 will create the smallest presentation and be the fastest to load.

Collaborate with Others

You can enlist the help of others in reviewing or editing your presentations when you use collaboration features. You can safeguard your presentation by requiring a password in order to view it. You can also use new Information Rights Management to not only control access to a presentation, but control how the presentation can be used by those you do authorize to open it.

You can send presentations to others in e-mail messages to review, and when they are finished editing the presentations, they can easily return them to you. Reviewers' edits are easy to identify and then act upon, and you can even consolidate multiple versions of your presentation and see who made each change to it. You can also use comments to add notes to presentations without changing the content itself.

You can now send presentations to others for review as shared attachments. Shared attachments are stored on a central Web server running Windows SharePoint Services as a shared workspace. When users receive your presentation in an e-mail message, they are prompted to check to see if there is a more current version on the shared workspace, which assures that each user is working with the latest version of your presentation.

You can access and modify resources on your shared workspace from within PowerPoint. You can use your shared workspace to view document version information. You can even sign up to receive an e-mail message when anything on your shared workspace changes.

Quick Tips

You can keep your presentation from being opened by unauthorized users when you assign a password to it. You can require one password for opening a presentation and another for editing a presentation. For example, if your presentation includes confidential sales information, you could require a password in order to open it.

Similarly, if you have a presentation you want certain users to be able make changes to and then save, you can create another password for the right to make changes to the presentation and then save them.

① Click Tools.

② Click Options.

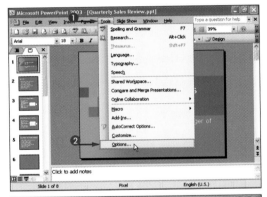

The Options dialog box appears.

③ Click the Security tab.

④ In the Password to open field, type the password for opening presentations.

⑤ In the Password to modify field, type the password for modifying presentations.

⑥ Click OK.

The Confirm Password dialog box appears.

⑦ In the Reenter password to open field, retype the password for opening presentations.

⑧ Click OK to confirm the password for opening the presentation.

The Confirm Password dialog box appears.

⑨ In the Reenter password to modify field, retype the password for modifying presentations.

⑩ Click OK to confirm the password for editing the presentation.

The Confirm Password and Options dialog boxes close. The passwords for opening and modifying the presentation are set for the presentation.

Caution!

Users can share passwords with others. For example, if you send the presentation attached to an e-mail message and include the password in the message body, the user can easily forward the message to someone else.

Information Rights Management (IRM) allows only designated users with the appropriate credentials who are logged either into Passport or into your company's network to access a presentation. IRM uses the Windows Rights Management service in Windows Server 2003 that helps companies set policies for how users can access and distribute company resources. If your company has not yet deployed Windows Server 2003 and IRM, you can still use it by subscribing to the Microsoft Office Online Service.

① Click File.

② Click Permission.

③ Click Restrict Permission As.

The Select User dialog box opens.

④ Click the user account you want to use.

⑤ Click OK.

The Permission dialog box appears.

⑥ Click the Restrict permission to this presentation option (☐ changes to ☑).

⑦ In the Read section, type the e-mail addresses of people who have read access to this presentation.

⑧ In the Change section, type the e-mail addresses of people with permission to change this presentation.

⑨ Click OK.

The restricted access rights are set and listed in the Shared Workspace Task Pane.

Did You Know?

To use IRM, you must first access the IRM service. This is done by specifying your Microsoft Passport e-mail address when you use Office Online. You can specify your Windows account name, such as DOMAIN/alias, when you use your company's service.

Send for Review allows you to send your presentation to others via e-mail message attachments. When you use Send for Review, your e-mail client is automatically opened with a message prepared with the presentation attached. Once you have addressed the message and included message content, you send the message. When the presentation is sent for review in an e-mail message, change tracking is automatically enabled so that changes the recipient makes to the presentation are flagged. When you open a presentation that has been edited by another person and change tracking has been enabled, you are asked if you want to merge the changes into your presentation.

SEND PRESENTATION FOR REVIEW

① Click File.

② Click Send To.

③ Click Mail Recipient (for Review).

Your e-mail client opens with a new message with the presentation attached.

④ Type the e-mail addresses of the people you want to send the presentation to for review.

⑤ Type any desired text in the body of the e-mail message.

⑥ Click Send.

An e-mail message is sent to each recipient with the presentation attached and revisions turned on.

OPEN REVIEWED PRESENTATION

① Double-click the presentation you want to open.

Note: You can also open the presentation in a network location by double-clicking it in Windows Explorer.

The Microsoft Office PowerPoint dialog box appears.

② Click Yes when asked if you want to merge changes back into the presentation.

The presentation opens in PowerPoint and the Reviewing toolbar and the Revisions Task Pane appear.

TIP

Did You Know?
When you use Send for Review, the Please review the attached document text is automatically inserted into the message. Because you will likely be sending a presentation, not a document, you might want to change that text to better suit your message.

When you open a presentation that has been edited by others, you are asked whether you want to merge changes with your original presentation. When you do so, the presentation opens with the Revisions Task Pane and the Reviewing toolbar visible. The Reviewing toolbar helps you quickly find the next change made in the presentation; the Revisions

Task Pane helps you find out who made the change and exactly what was changed.

When multiple changes have been made on a slide, you can choose which changes you want to apply. This is important when you receive contradictory or conflicting comments from reviewers.

---

1 Double-click the presentation you want to open.

Note: You can also open the presentation from a network location by double-clicking it in Windows Explorer.

The Microsoft Office PowerPoint dialog box appears.

2 Click Yes when asked if you want to merge changes back into the presentation.

The presentation opens in PowerPoint, and the Reviewing toolbar and the Revisions Task Pane appear.

3 On the Reviewing toolbar, click the Next Item button.

The Slide changes section in the Revisions Task Pane lists the revisions made on the slide.

④ Click the revision you want to review.

The revisions details list appears.

⑤ Click the option for the revisions you want to accept (☐ changes to ☑).

The selected revisions are made in the slide.

⑥ On the Reviewing toolbar, click the Next Item button.

The next revision appears in the Revisions Task Pane.

⑦ Click the revision you want to review.

⑧ Click the option for the revision you want to reject (☐ changes to ☑).

⑨ On the Reviewing toolbar, click the Unapply button.

The revision is removed from the slide.

⑩ Repeat steps **3** to **9** until all revisions have been addressed.

Did You Know?

When you reject, or Unapply, a revision, you are choosing not to include it in a presentation. When you accept a revision, you are choosing to use it in the presentation.

Comments can be a great way to communicate with a presentation's author without changing the presentation itself. Comments inserted into a slide are displayed with a different color for each reviewer. They also display the name of the reviewer who made the comment and the date the comment was inserted or edited. When the comments are not opened, a small colored box is displayed that shows the initials of the person who inserted the comment plus a number. This allows one person to insert more than one comment on a page, such as NAB1, NAB2, and NAB3.

INSERT A NEW COMMENT

① Click Insert.

② Click Comment.

A blank comment is inserted into the slide.

③ Click the comment form, and then type your comments.

④ Click off the comment on the slide.

The comment form closes but the comment symbol remains.

⑤ Right-click the comment symbol.

The content menu appears.

⑥ Click Edit Comment.

The comment form appears.

⑦ Click and then type to edit the comment.

Name It!

You can change the name and initials that are displayed in Comments. Click Tools, and then Options. In the Options dialog box, click the General tab, change the name in the Name field, and then the initials in the Initials field. Click OK. Future Comments will use the new name and initials.

You can save time and make the revisions process easier by combining all revised presentations from co-workers when you use Compare and Merge Presentations. When multiple presentations are merged, the Reviewing toolbar and the Revisions Task Pane appear. The Reviewing toolbar makes it easy to find each revision, and the Revisions Task Pane allows you to see

a list of the changes and who made them. The Revisions Task Pane also allows you to see a list of changes made to the presentation overall. You can use the Reviewing toolbar to choose to accept all changes made to a slide or to the entire presentation.

① Click Tools.

② Click Compare and Merge Presentations.

The Choose Files to Merge with Current Presentation dialog box appears.

③ Click here and select the folder in which the presentations you want to merge with this presentation are located.

④ Press Ctrl+click to select all of the files you want to merge with this presentation.

⑤ Click Merge.

The presentations are merged, and the Revisions Task Pane and the Reviewing toolbar appear.

⑥ On the Reviewing toolbar, click the Next Item button to review changes.

⑦ Click the Apply · on the Reviewing toolbar.

⑧ Click Apply All Changes to the Presentation.

All changes are made to the presentations.

⑨ Click End Review.

The Reviewing toolbar closes and the review cycle is finished.

Did You Know?

Compare and Merge Presentations compares presentations against the presentation that is currently open. Start by opening the presentation to which you want to compare other versions of the presentations.

By sending presentations as e-mail attachments, you can save time. Instead of finding a network location that all recipients have access to and then sending an e-mail message requesting updates to the presentation, you can instead just send the presentation via e-mail. It also saves time to use Send To Mail Recipient as Attachment because it attaches the

presentation to the e-mail message for you. Without Send To Mail Recipient as Attachment, you would have to open your e-mail client, start a new e-mail message, and attach the presentation to the message. These steps are taken care of when you use Send To Mail Recipient as Attachment.

① Click File.

② Click Send To.

③ Click Mail Recipient (as Attachment).

Your e-mail client opens with a new mail message created with the presentation attached.

④ Click To.

The Select Names dialog box appears.

⑤ In the Name section, click the name of those to whom you want to send the presentation.

Note: If you want to send to more than one person, press Ctrl+click to select more than one name.

⑥ Click To.

⑦ Click OK.

⑧ Type your message in the body of the e-mail message.

⑨ Click Send.

The message is sent with the presentation attached.

Caution!

You should use caution when you use e-mail to send large presentations. Some recipients may use e-mail providers that limit the size of attachments. Additionally, users with low bandwidth connections may not want to wait for large presentations to download when they check for e-mail.

Unlike presentations sent as regular attachments, shared attachments are stored on a central Web server running Windows Server 2003. Each shared attachment is stored on a separate Document Workspace, which you can think of as a Web site where team members can collaborate.

When you send a presentation as a shared attachment, you specify the path to the Web server, and information about the Document Workspace is automatically inserted into an e-mail message with a link to the Document Workspace. The presentation is also inserted into the e-mail message. Once the presentation is sent, the Document Workspace is automatically created and a copy of the presentation is stored on it.

① Click File.

② Click Send To.

③ Click Mail Recipient (as Attachment).

Your e-mail client opens with a new mail message created with the presentation attached.

④ Type the desired text in the body of the e-mail message.

⑤ Click To.

The Select Names dialog box appears.

6 In the Name section press Ctrl+click to select the names of those to whom you want to send the shared attachment.

7 Click To.

8 Click OK.

The Select Names dialog box closes.

9 Click Attachment Options.

The Attachment Options Task Pane appears.

10 Click the Shared attachments option (○ changes to ◉).

11 Click the Create Document Workspace at field and type the URL of the Web site.

12 Click Send.

The Document Workspace is provisioned, and the e-mail message is sent with the presentation attached.

Attention!

Before you attempt this task, find out if your company has a Web server running Windows Server 2003 and Windows SharePoint Services. If it does, you need to ask the server administrator to grant you rights to create Document Workspaces. Upon granting you rights, the administrator will give you the URL to the server that you will need to perform step **11** above.

When you double-click a presentation that you have received as a shared attachment, you are prompted to check to see if there is a more recent version. If you choose to get updates, PowerPoint checks the version posted in the Document Workspace. If the version you are using is not the most current version, you are asked if you want to instead open the

more recent version from the server. Once you make your edits and save them, you are prompted to save your changes to the Document Workspace. Then, anyone who opens the shared document is prompted to open your more recent version from the Document Workspace.

① Double-click the shared attachment.

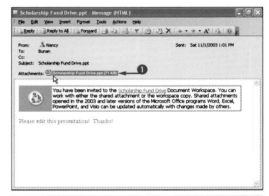

Note: *If a dialog box appears asking if you want to open the attachment, click Open.*

The Microsoft Office PowerPoint dialog box appears.

② Click Get Updates.

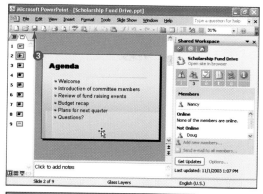

The most recent version of the presentation opens in PowerPoint, and the Shared Workspace Task Pane appears.

You can make edits to the presentation.

③ Click Save.

A notice appears in the Shared Workspace Task Pane asking if you want to update the presentation in the Shared Workspace.

④ Click Update Workspace Copy.

The presentation is updated in the Shared Workspace.

Attention!

The Status tab on the Shared Workspace Task Pane displays an alert when the version of the presentation with which you are working is no longer the most current. You can also click the Get Updates button on any tab to get a more recent version of the presentation.

Document Workspaces are Web sites that are provisioned for you to store documents and document information, lists of links, lists of team members, and tasks. Document Workspaces rely on Windows Server 2003 and Windows SharePoint Services, and you must have access rights in order to create Shared Workspaces. The Shared Workspaces Task Pane gives you a view of each Document Workspace without leaving PowerPoint to go to your browser. When you create a new Document Workspace from the Shared Workspaces Task Pane, it creates the Document Workspace on the server, and then includes a hyperlink to it in the Shared Workspaces Task Pane.

① Click View.

② Click Task Pane.

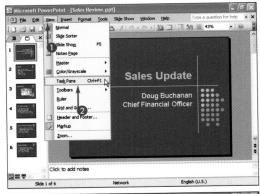

The PowerPoint Help Task Pane appears.

③ Click the Task Pane ▼.

④ Click Shared Workspace.

The Shared Workspace
Task Pane appears.

⑤ Click the Location for
new workspace field,
and type the URL of the
Web site for which you
want to create the
Document Workspace.

⑥ Click Create.

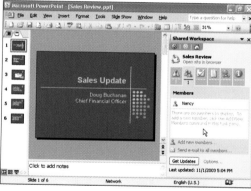

The Document
Workspace is
provisioned for you and
reflected in the Shared
Workspace Task Pane.

More Options!
You can also make changes to your Document Workspace from the
browser. To access the Document Workspace in the browser, click the
Open site in browser link on the Shared Workspace Task Pane to open
the Shared Workspace in the browser.

You can use a Document Workspace to keep all related documents in one place. For example, if you have already created a presentation on budget plans for the next year and have stored it on a Document Workspace, you may also want to store a budget spreadsheet or policy document there as well. You can add documents to an existing Document Workspace by first

opening the presentation that is already stored in the Document Workspace to which you want to add documents. When that presentation opens, the Shared Workspace Task Pane appears and displays the contents of the Document Workspace. You can then upload additional documents.

① **Open the presentation that is stored in the Document Workspace to which you want to add a presentation.**

② **Click Tools.**

③ **Click Shared Workspace.**

The Shared Workspace Task Pane appears.

④ **Click the Documents button.**

⑤ **Click Add new document.**

The Add New Document dialog box appears.

6 In the File Name field, type the path to the file that you want to upload to the Document Workspace.

7 Click OK.

The presentation uploads to the Document Workspace.

More Options!

You can also browse to a file to upload it instead of typing a path. Follow the steps above, but in step **6**, click the Browse button. The Choose file dialog box appears. Click the Look in 🔽 and then click the folder in which the file is located. Click the file you want to add to the Document Workspace, and then click Open. Then proceed with step **7**.

You can change who has access to a Document Workspace in which your presentation is stored without leaving PowerPoint. Because each Document Workspace is a Web site, making sure that team members have access rights is essential. When you add team members to a Document Workspace, they can

be added by their user name, Windows domain and user name, or by e-mail address. However, if you enter users by their e-mail address, they must also have a Windows account on the server running the Document Workspace.

① **Open the presentation that is stored in the Document Workspace to which you want to add new members.**

Note: *If asked if you want to get the latest version from the Document Workspace, click Get Updates.*

② **Click the Members button.**

③ **Click Add new members.**

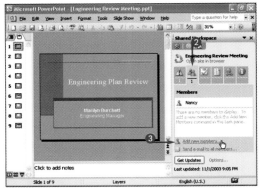

The Add New Members dialog box appears.

④ **In the Enter e-mail addresses or user names field, type the e-mail addresses or Windows domain and user names.**

Note: *If you have multiple users to add, separate them with semicolons.*

⑤ **Click Next.**

The next Add New Members dialog box appears.

6 Verify that the user names, e-mail addresses, and display names are the way you want them. If not, make desired changes.

Note: *This is your last chance to change this information before adding it to the Web site.*

7 Click Finish.

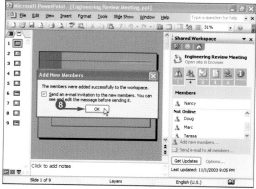

The next Add New Members dialog box appears.

8 Click OK.

New members are sent an e-mail message welcoming them to the Document Workspace, and they are listed in the Shared Workspace Task Pane.

Did You Know?

When you create a Document Workspace by sending a presentation as a shared attachment, all of the people to whom the e-mail message is addressed are added to the Document Workspace. When you create a Document Workspace from the Shared Workspace Task Pane, you are the only team member added.

When you save a presentation to a Document Workspace, version information is automatically saved with it, such as the dates on which it was saved, and by whom. Version history is especially useful when you are responsible for presentations that are being edited by multiple users. The ability to find out who modified each version of the presentation

makes each team member accountable and helps give you confidence in delegating presentation work to others.

Version information is accessible from the Document Information tab on the Shared Workspace Task Pane. Version information displayed includes version number, date modified, by whom it was modified, the size, and comments.

① Open the presentation of which you want to check the revision history.

The Microsoft Office PowerPoint dialog box appears.

② Click Get Updates.

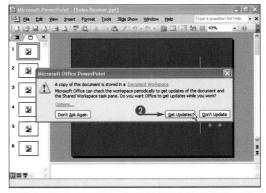

The presentation opens with the Shared Workspace Task Pane opened.

③ Click the Document Information button.

Document information appears in the Shared Workspace Task Pane.

④ Click Version history.

The Versions saved dialog box appears.

⑤ Click the version if you want to open that presentation.

⑥ Click Close.

Caution!

Versioning is very useful if your documents are important and you need the ability to roll back a presentation to a previous version. However, because a copy of each version is saved every time the presentation is saved, it means that each version takes up more hard disk space on your server. Therefore, you might want to routinely delete versions that you no longer need to keep. You can delete unneeded versions by following steps **1** to **5** above, and then clicking Delete.

You can stay updated on documents in your Document Workspace when you request alerts. When you are anxiously awaiting feedback from team members on a presentation, it is tempting to continually check the Document Workspace for updates. Instead, you can request an alert, which is an e-mail message that is automatically generated

from the server, telling you that your document has changed.

You can choose to receive an e-mail alert when anything changes in the Document Workspace. You can also specify how often you would like to receive alerts, such as weekly, daily, or directly after the Document Workspace changes.

---

① Open the presentation from which you want to receive alerts.

The Microsoft Office PowerPoint dialog box appears.

② Click Get Updates.

The presentation opens with the Shared Workspace Task Pane opened.

③ Click the Document Information button.

④ Click the Alert me about this document link.

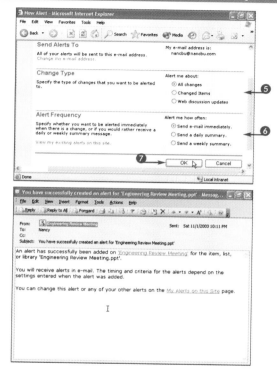

The browser opens to the New Alert page on the Document Workspace Web site.

⑤ Click the option for the type of changes to which you want to receive alerts (○ changes to ◉).

⑥ Click the option for the frequency in which you want to receive alerts (○ changes to ◉).

⑦ Click OK.

Your request for alerts is accepted, and you are automatically sent a confirmation e-mail message.

Save It!

The confirmation e-mail message you receive after signing up for alerts contains a link to the alerts administration page. This link is also sent in alert e-mail messages in case you want to change the frequency of alerts or even cancel your alerts subscription.

Document Workspaces are displayed in PowerPoint on the Shared Workspace Task Pane. The Links tab, also displayed on the Shared Workspace Task Pane, allows you to add hyperlinks to direct Document Workspace users to related Web sites and documents stored on your company's network.

For example, in a Document Workspace created for a presentation about new products, you could include hyperlinks to the product's marketing plan, to the product's Web site, and to a competitor's Web site, all from within the Shared Workspace Task Pane. When the visitor clicks one of the links, either the visitor's browser opens or the document or program linked to is launched.

① Open the presentation in the Shared Workspace to which you want to add links.

The Microsoft Office PowerPoint dialog box appears.

② Click Get Updates.

The presentation opens with the Shared Workspace Task Pane opened.

③ Click the Links button.

④ Click Add new link.

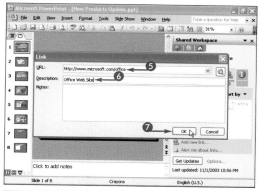

The Link dialog box appears.

⑤ In the URL field, type the URL for the hyperlink.

⑥ In the Description field, type the text you want to appear in the Links list.

⑦ Click OK.

The hyperlink is added to the Links list.

Did You Know?

You can also browse to the Web site to which you wish to link if you do not know its URL. In step **5** above, click the Browse button (🔍) on the Link dialog box, and your browser opens. Browse to the Web page to which you want to link, and then return to PowerPoint. The URL is automatically inserted in the URL field. Proceed with step **6** to complete adding the link.

Deliver and Distribute Your Presentation Effectively

You can deliver effective presentations regardless of whether your audience is live or your presentations are available for off-line or unattended use. You can create a custom show that displays only a subset of the slides in a presentation. You can hide slides so that they do not display during presentation unless you specifically bring them up.

You can use Rehearse Timings to practice your presentation and determine how long it will take to present each slide. You can even program your presentation to replay after the last slide when you need to repeat a presentation.

If you have a Tablet PC, you can use your pen input device to draw on your Tablet PC screen and display that ink directly on your slides.

You can create presentations for viewers to play in your absence by creating a kiosk presentation. Kiosk presentations play in Slide Show Mode and advance automatically to the next slide. You can even burn your presentation to a CD and make it available for use by viewers who do not have PowerPoint.

Quick Tips

Create a Custom Show Instead of a New Presentation

Custom slide shows are collections of slides in a presentation that you can play together. For example, if you have a large presentation that outlines your company's products and services, you may want to create a custom show that displays only slides about new products. When it is time to deliver your presentation, you can choose the custom show to play in Slide Show Mode. Without custom shows, you would probably have to create a different version of the presentation for each audience or for each use. When you create custom shows, you keep all of the slides in the same presentation, which saves time and simplifies updating.

① Click Slide Show.

② Click Custom Shows.

The Custom Shows dialog box appears.

③ Click New.

The Define Custom Show dialog box appears.

④ In the Slide show name field, type the name for this slide show.

⑤ In the Slides in presentation section, click a slide that you want to add to the custom show.

⑥ Click Add to add the slide to your custom show list.

⑦ Repeat steps **5** and **6** until your list contains all the slides you want to include in the custom show.

⑧ Click OK.

The Define Custom Show dialog box closes, and the Custom Shows dialog box is again visible.

⑨ Click Show to view your custom presentation.

Your presentation plays in Slide Show Mode with the slides you have chosen.

Did You Know?

You can also create custom shows as a way to reorder slides for a given audience. For example, if presentation time is limited, you can create a custom show that presents your most important slides first in case you run out of time.

You can include slides in your presentation that do not print in handouts or display in presentations unless you specifically bring them up. These slides are called hidden slides, and they can be very useful when you have material that you may need to present, but are not sure. You can use hidden slides when you have a time limit and are not sure whether you can complete all slides during a given time period.

Flagging slides as hidden is easy. When you give your presentation, the hidden slides are omitted unless you use Go To Slide to advance to a hidden slide.

HIDE SLIDES

1. Click View.
2. Click Slide Sorter.

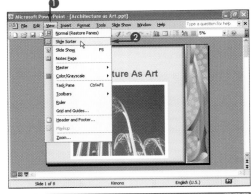

The presentation appears in Slide Sorter View.

3. Right-click the slide you want to hide.

The content menu appears.

4. Click Hide Slide.
5. Repeat steps 3 and 4 for all the slides you want to hide.

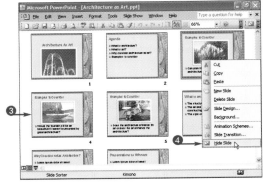

VIEW HIDDEN SLIDES DURING SLIDE SHOW

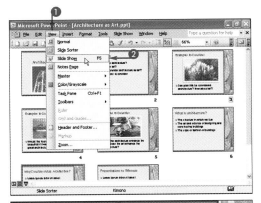

1 Click View.

2 Click Slide Show.

The presentation opens in Slide Show Mode.

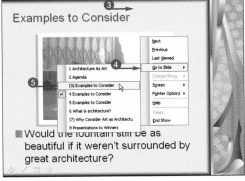

3 Right-click the slide.

The content menu appears.

4 Click Go to Slide.

The list of slides appears.

5 Click the hidden slide you want to view.

The hidden slide opens.

TIP

Did You Know?

When you use Go to Slide during a presentation, hidden slides are shown with the slide number in parentheses. For example, a non-hidden slide might appear as 2 Agenda, while a hidden slide might appear as (2) Agenda.

You can practice your presentation and record the amount of time each slide needs when you use Rehearse. When you use Rehearse Timings, your presentation is displayed in Slide Show Mode, and the Rehearsal toolbar is displayed. Every time you advance to the next slide, the time you spent on the previous slide is recorded.

Rehearse Timings is also a good way to assign times to slides that you use in unattended presentations. For example, if you create a kiosk presentation, slides in the presentation advance using the timings set when you use Rehearse Timings.

① Click Slide Show.

② Click Rehearse Timings.

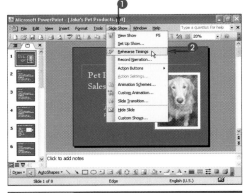

The Rehearsal toolbar appears.

③ Click Next to advance to the next slide.

④ Repeat step **3** for all of the slides in your presentation.

After the last slide in the presentation, the Microsoft Office PowerPoint dialog box appears, asking if you want to keep the slide timing for future use.

⑤ Click Yes.

The presentation appears in Slide Sorter View with the slide timings noted under each slide.

Pause It!
If you are interrupted while rehearsing a presentation, you can click the Pause button (⏸) on the Rehearsal toolbar. The timings stop until you click the Play button (⏵).

You can set up your presentation to replay continuously by moving from the last slide back to the first slide in your presentation. The ability to loop presentations is especially useful when you have to repeat a presentation without interruption between sessions. Without the ability to continually loop the presentation, when you finish delivering

your presentation in Slide Show Mode, the presentation goes back to Normal View in PowerPoint, which you would not want the audience to see. When you continually loop the presentation, you can advance from the last slide to the first without interruption because the presentation stays in Slide Show Mode the entire time.

① Click Slide Show.

② Click Set Up Show.

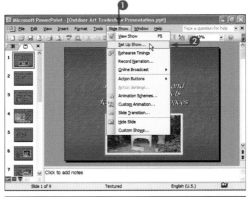

The Set Up Show dialog box appears.

③ In the Show options section, click the Loop continuously until 'Esc' option (☐ changes to ☑).

④ In the Advance slides section, click the Manually option (○ changes to ◉).

⑤ Click OK.

The slide show is set to repeat continuously until you press the Esc key.

6 Click View.

7 Click Slide Show.

The presentation plays continuously in Slide Show Mode. That is, after the last slide in the show appears, the first slide reappears, playing the presentation repeatedly without interruption.

Did You Know?

You can choose to use slide timings instead of manually advancing each slide. Follow the steps above, but in step 4 click the Using timings, if present option (○ changes to ◉) instead of the Manually option (◉ changes to ○).

If you are a Tablet PC computer user, you can use your pen input device to add free-form notes and annotations to your slides while you give a presentation. The Tablet PC pen input device allows you to draw on your computer screen, and your drawings are enhanced with colorful lines that look like they are part of the slides.

When you view your presentation in Slide Show Mode, you can tap the pen symbol with your pen input device to see the options available while working with ink during your presentation. Options include changing pen type and changing the color of the ink itself.

① Click View.

② Click Slide Show.

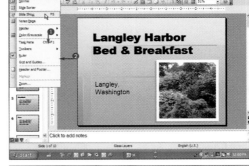

The presentation opens in Slide Show Mode.

③ With your pen input device, tap Pen.

The Pen symbol becomes visible.

④ Tap Pen again.

The content menu appears.

⑤ Tap Ink Color.

⑥ In the palette that appears, tap the ink color that you want to use.

⑦ Proceed with your presentation, using ink to annotate the slides as desired.

Try This!

You can choose the primary ink color for a presentation before you enter Slide Show Mode. Click Slide Show and then Set Up Show. In the Set Up Show dialog box, click the Pen Color ⬇, select the color you want to use, and then click OK.

Create a Kiosk Presentation That Runs Unattended

Kiosk presentations play full screen in Slide Show Mode repeatedly until interrupted, and are ideal when you want viewers to see your presentation but are not physically present to advance slides or restart the presentation when it is complete. Kiosk presentations rely on slide timings to determine when a slide should advance. Slide timings are set by using Rehearse Timings, which records the amount of time you spend on each slide. When your presentation plays, slides advance according to the times set when you rehearsed your presentation. Once the presentation enters Slide Show Mode, it continues to play until the Esc key is pressed.

① Click Slide Show.

② Click Rehearse Timings.

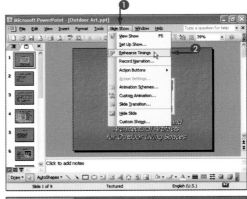

The presentation opens in Slide Show Mode, and the Rehearsal toolbar appears.

③ Click Next when it is the right time to advance to the next slide.

④ Repeat step **3** until timings have been assigned to all the slides in the presentation.

The presentation returns to Normal View.

5 Click Slide Show.

6 Click Set Up Show.

The Set Up Show dialog box appears.

7 In the Show type section, click the Browsed at a kiosk (full screen) option (◯ changes to ◉).

8 In the Advance slides section, click the Use timings, if present option (◯ changes to ◉).

9 Click OK.

The next time you enter Slide Show Mode, the presentation will advance automatically using the timings you set and will continually repeat after it is finished.

Did You Know?

Kiosk presentations work well with multimedia content. For example, presentations with slide transitions, audio, video, and animations can be more attention getting than plain presentations, and work well in kiosk mode.

Play Your Presentation in PowerPoint Viewer

You can make your presentation available to viewers even if they are not PowerPoint users by recommending the use of the PowerPoint 2003 Viewer. The PowerPoint 2003 Viewer is a program that is available free from the Microsoft Download Center.

A convenient way to get the PowerPoint 2003 Viewer is to use Package for CD, but instead export the files to a folder from which you can copy the Viewer and the presentation. You can attach these files to an e-mail message or post them on a shared network for others to access.

---

① Click File.

② Click Package for CD.

The Package for CD dialog box appears.

③ Type the name of the CD.

④ Click Copy to Folder.

The Copy to Folder dialog box appears.

⑤ Type the name for the folder.

⑥ Type the path of the folder to which you want to copy your files.

⑦ Click OK.

The files necessary to burn your presentation to CD, including the PowerPoint Viewer file, are created.

⑧ Open the Windows Explorer to the directory you specified in steps **6** and **7**.

● The PowerPoint Viewer and all of the files needed to view the presentation are available for distribution.

Important!
The PowerPoint 2003 Viewer is designed for playing back presentations that have been created with PowerPoint 97 or later. Users of the PowerPoint Viewer 2003 can view presentations, but they cannot edit them.

Burn a Presentation CD for a Wider Distribution

You can make your presentation available to a larger audience when you burn it to a CD and then distribute it. Package for CD makes it easy and automatic to package and then burn all of the files that are needed directly onto a CD. PowerPoint 2003 simplifies the CD creation process. Assign a name to the CD, and then instruct PowerPoint to copy the files to the CD. PowerPoint communicates with your computer's CD burner to copy your presentation onto the CD. When the recipient inserts the CD into his or her CD drive, it automatically opens the PowerPoint 2003 Viewer and plays the presentation.

---

① Click File.

② Click Package for CD.

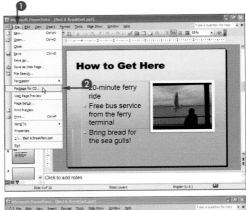

The Package for CD dialog box appears.

③ Type the name of the CD.

④ Click Copy to CD.

The Copying Files to CD dialog box appears, displaying a progress indicator on the status of your action. When the process completes, the Microsoft Office PowerPoint dialog box appears.

⑤ Click No.

⑥ Open Windows Explorer to view your completed CD.

● All the files you need for viewing the presentation are on the CD.

Try This!

You can add additional files to the CD if you want. For example, if you are creating a CD that contains a presentation about new products, you might want to also include a product brochure or price list. Follow steps **1** to **3** above, and then click Add Files on the Package for CD dialog box.

Index

Index

Index